DURHAM CATHEDRAL

AN ARCHITECTURAL APPRECIATION

DOUGLAS POCOCK   MALCOLM THURLBY

DAVID PARK   IAN CURRY

Durham: City of Durham Trust

© City of Durham Trust

First published 2014 by
City of Durham Trust

Typeset and printed by Azure Printing
Pegswood, Morpeth, NE61 6HZ

ISBN 0 902776 12 6

Contents

Introduction and Acknowledgements

Durham Cathedral is a structure universally acknowledged by both past travellers and present tourist agencies, by both artists and, not least, by architects. It is a work of art, a cultural benchmark and an engineering feat in the evolution of western civilisation. The last-mentioned quality is the justification for this brief volume, which is devoted the architecture of a unique building, one by which others are judged. The niche for such a volume was suggested by the on-site cathedral bookshop.

The four authors, all of whom have written about the Cathedral before, in sequence of their chapters are: Douglas Pocock, Reader Emeritus in Geography in Durham University and Secretary of the City of Durham Trust; Malcolm Thurlby, Professor of Art and Architectural History at York University, Toronto; Professor David Park, Director of Conservation of Wall Painting Department at the Courtauld Institute of Art; Ian Curry, Consultant Architect to the Dean and Chapter of Durham from 1976-1997, and also a Member of the Cathedral Commission for England. (Ian died in 2012; his essay reprinted here has been updated to include most recent changes.)

All authors are indebted to the Chapter of Durham Cathedral for permission to publish all the photographs of the interior of the Cathedral. The illustrations of Figures 53-58 are also the copyright of the Chapter of Durham Cathedral. Figure 1 is reproduced by permission of Durham County Council. Philip Davies, Chapter Clerk, kindly arranged the most recent photographic reconnaissances by Malcolm Thurlby, the results of which are seen in Chapter 2 and the front cover.

Douglas Pocock

1. Appreciation of 'the best building in the world'

Durham Cathedral received the appellation 'the best building in the world' in 1984. The assessment was made by some fifty experts, who were commissioned by *Illustrated London News* to assess the world's leading man-made constructions on the occasion of the 150th anniversary of the Royal Institute of British Architects. [1] Durham Cathedral was a convincing winner, ahead even of the Taj Mahal and Parthenon, which were in second and third places, respectively. Notwithstanding any charge of ethnocentrism, the cathedral is certainly worthy of inclusion in the annals of architecture. It was the UK's first cathedral to be inscribed on UNESCO's list of World Heritage Sites, and is noted not only for its innovative nature, but for beauty of form and setting, besides its cultural significance.

Origins of the Norman Cathedral

The present cathedral is to be seen within the context of the cultural evolution of the North East, set within the broader political history of the country as a whole. The conquering Normans succeeded to, or confirmed, the site which had been chosen in 995 by a peripatetic Anglo-Saxon religious community. The latter had been forced from their home on Lindisfarne, or Holy Island, by Viking invaders in 875, taking with them the uncorrupt body of St Cuthbert, a holy man and miracle-worker, not least after his death, together with gifts and treasures that had been offered to the saint. When the raised, river-girt, defensive site at Durham was eventually chosen, a stone cathedral was erected to house the shrine of England's most famous saint. Sufficient building had taken place by 999, when his body was enshrined, although the structure was not completed until 1017. The bones of St Bede were soon added and further gifts of land accepted, such that Durham was now conveniently located with regard to the Community's extensive estates. [2]

The Normans took advantage of both site and general situation, for Durham offered the first defensive site north of the river Tees suitable as a centre from which to control the northern outpost of their new kingdom. Having taken cognisance of the Church's organisation, along with St Cuthbert's significance in the region, William the Conqueror confirmed the lands, laws and liberties of the Church and in 1071 installed the first in a line of non-hereditary bishops. The latter were to become prince-bishops, the monarch's regent in a palatinate with secular as well as spiritual powers.

The second prince-bishop, William of St Calais (bp 1081-96) was to play the crucial role in the creation of the building we see today. In addition to being patron and paymaster for the cathedral, it is possible that he was also responsible for the design brief, master mason, notwithstanding. He had had experience of the Romanesque architecture and structural advances on the continent, as well as being aware of the dozen cathedrals or abbeys built or begun in southern and midland England since the Conquest, which, together with his visit to Rome, crystallised into a vision to emulate the best in Europe.

Scale, layout, vaulting and decoration were thus combined in a monumental essay. Symbolically, the overall length, width and apsidal east end were identical to that of (old) St

Fig. 1. 'The building of Durham,' (detail) by Thomas Pattinson, 1963, County Hall, Durham

Peter's in Rome, with spiral columns reserved for the vicinity of St Cuthbert's shrine to replicate that of Christianity's leading saint. Unsurprisingly, St Cuthbert was included in the designation of the cathedral

The foundation stones of the new cathedral were laid in 1093 by Bishop William of St Calais and Prior Turgot, the former having ordered the demolition of the Anglo-Saxon cathedral one year before. (The latter building had stood for fewer than eighty years.) Work continued after the bishop's death three years later so that by the time a successor was appointed - Bishop Rannulph Flambard, (bp 1099-1128) - the building had advanced as far as the nave. In 1104 the body of St Cuthbert was translated from what remained of the Anglo-Saxon church to a shrine behind the high altar. The work continued, ever westwards, finishing in 1133. On the evidence of masons' marks, approaching 200 craftsmen were engaged in building the greatest church in England, and one of the greatest in Europe (Fig.1). The task had been completed in forty years.

The vast amount of stone for the building was obtained locally. The Low Main Post, or Cathedral, Sandstone, which is readily masoned, occurs in the river gorge, up to 35 feet in thickness. Evidence of early quarries are visible today – as are indications that in places working approached too close to the lip of the gorge. Witness the buttresses needed to clamp the Galilee Chapel to the plateau edge, and in the name, 'Broken Walls'. The great bulk of the stone almost certainly came from just across the river, beyond South Street, the resultant declivity later becoming the abbey fishpond and orchard. One interesting aspect of the masons' work is that the blocks constituting the boldly incised patterns of the cylindrical piers were individually prefabricated before being assembled in the cathedral. [3]

The Romanesque Cathedral considered

The uninterrupted view of the north elevation across Palace Green will almost certainly be the visitor's first sight of the cathedral, it having suddenly opened up at the head of the short cobbled rise of Owengate. The classical form, with a dominant crossing tower balanced by western towers and eastern transept, loses its apparent symmetry with more detailed observation. Post-Romanesque features also become evident, most notably the 15th century central tower, which reveals a two-stage progression. The western towers received their present open parapet around 1800, while some Early English fenestration is also evident.

Further discussion of the exterior will not be pursued here. (Anyone who is interested in examining the exterior is strongly advised to include a night-time perambulation, when the illumination highlights details not readily appreciated by day.) Here, we will follow the advice of Sherban Cantacuzino, who reminds us that "the inside matters more than the outside, for medieval churches were conceived from the inside out." [4]

After completion in 1133 William of St Calais' master design did not undergo changes or additions to the extent of other post-Conquest cathedrals; it is not therefore a repository of architectural styles, but remains essentially Romanesque in form and detail. Two major features, however, are to be borne in mind when engaging with the building today. One is that the warm, natural colour of the sandstone, which is so appealing today, was originally painted. (This colour was itself covered by white-wash in the 17th century, and removed only in the latter half of the 19th century.) A trained eye will detect isolated remnants of the original decorative colouring; a small reconstruction in the dado arcade in the south aisle of the nave gives an indication of the former decoration.

The second original feature was a stone screen across the front of the nave, thus shutting off the chancel from view. [5] (Damage marks on the two western compound piers of the crossing indicate the former position of the screen.) After its removal, a heavily-carved wooden screen, with organ above, between the two eastern compound piers, continued a visual block until the mid 19th century. The present triple arched screen by George Gilbert Scott (1876) does away with any visual blockage although at the same time signifying a division of space The eye is therefore attracted to the Neville Screen (1346), a delicate structure in Caen stone, with the rose window (1275, renewed 1800) rising behind. The former, by Henry Yevele, is the only example in England of a canopied reredos of its kind in Perpendicular style.

The initial reaction to the interior is likely to be the sheer massiveness of the building. The apparent Norman show of strength, which caused Sir Walter Scott to described the cathedral as "half church of God, half castle 'gainst the Scot", proves to be, in fact, more than poetic description in that the two western towers were originally integrated into the castle wall defending the western lip of the peninsula. Moreover, the width of the upper galleries could well suggest incorporation of a secondary military role.

Strength emanates from the piers, marching rhythmically eastwards, paired alternately round and compound. The massiveness of the round piers is lightened by deeply incised patterning;

working eastwards, successively, vertical fluting, chevron, lozenge and, finally, spiral (Fig.2). (In previous churches such patterns had been painted, not sculpted.) Further decoration was added to the nave when the arcades, gallery and clerestory, together with the vault ribs, were given chevron marking. The absence of decoration on the arcades of the first piers west of the crossing indicates how far the construction of the building had progressed before the arrival of Bishop Flambard and the decision to imprint with chevron was taken. Accordingly, there is a recognisable sequence west as the decoration extends downwards from the clerestory to the gallery and then to the arcade. (Less perceptible will be the fact that the distance between subsequent piers was an extra three paces, the increase necessary if the overall length of the building were to exactly replicate that of St Peter's.) The resultant decoration constitutes the earliest significant chevron ornamentation in this country and, possibly, in northern Europe. (It was later to become the dominant motive in the Galilee Chapel.)

Decorative, interlaced blind arcading, ten feet in height, binds together the outer walls of the side aisles and transepts Overall unity is provided by the pleasing proportions of arcade, gallery and clerestory, all in buff-coloured sandstone and extending the length of the building. Above, the composition is completed by a further sense of lightness as the eye is led eastwards by the high vault, with pairs of delicate stone ribs crossing each bay diagonally, and with pointed arches whispering of the Gothic which was to come. In the words of Conant, Durham "has the air of serene finality which belongs of right to great masterpieces." [6] Accordingly, Durham Cathedral is a building by which others are judged.

While the cathedral's pleasing proportions, unity of material and high degree of decoration constitute an aesthetic high, surpassing any of its contemporaries, it is renowned above all for its innovative architecture. Features just mentioned are the sculptured incisions on its piers, chevrons and blind arcading, but pre-eminent was the advance in architectural, or engineering, technology in tackling the thrust exerted by high stone vaults. While, independently, similar audacious vaulting was being attempted at Cluny in France and Speyer in Germany, Durham has claim to be the first major building to be entirely covered by stone ribbed vaulting with pointed arches. It was in this cathedral, then, that the pointed arch, as opposed to the groin variety, was first used successfully as a structural element, the arches rising across the nave from pilasters which constitute part of the compound piers. Stone ribbing provides additional support to the vault, while at the same time seeming to lighten the overall appearance. A graceful pattern is composed of ribs in each bay springing from the pilasters and intervening corbel-heads to form a double compartment of diagonal quadripartite rib vaulting.

Previously, wooden roofs had prevailed. With stone, a pointed arch was superior to a rounded one in that it allowed achievement of a greater height. The consequent thrust of the arched vaulting was transmitted to its massive pillars and walls. Lateral abutments, or quadrant arches, across the galleries were initially considered to be proto flying buttresses, but this is now discounted. It is now considered that they were originally related to the aisle roof rather than lateral thrust, even though they were strengthened in the Victorian era. (The addition of two inner orders to the quadrant arches have been dated to the early twentieth century. [7]) Nevertheless, it was in Durham that the structural thrust problem of the Gothic was resolved, albeit in a

Fig. 2.   Incised patterns on nave's cylindrical piers. Top left to bottom right - fluting, chevron, lozenge, spiral.

8

Romanesque construction. The achievement, according to Pevsner, was "the ultimate fulfilment of that tendency towards articulation which had driven Romanesque architects forward for over a hundred years." [8]

The first section of innovative vaulting was erected over the chancel in, or by, 1104, the year of St Cuthbert's translation. (It had to be replaced in the late 13th century, an indication perhaps of its experimental nature.) There is then evidence that a wooden ceiling was briefly considered before the north transept was vaulted in 1110; the south transept followed a few years later; the high vault of the nave was the last part of the cathedral to be completed between 1128-33.

Two extensions to the Norman Church

The cathedral as envisaged by William of St Calais and largely completed during the bishopric of Rannulph Flambard was given two significant additions by the attachment of chapels to both its west and east fronts, the Galilee Chapel and the Chapel of the Nine Altars, respectively.

The Galilee, or Lady, Chapel (1175-80) was the work of Bishop Hugh of Le Puiset (bp 1153-95). Initial attempts to incorporate a Lady Chapel at the east end of the cathedral were frustrated by cracks attributable to a greater depth of unconsolidated material as a result of gently eastward-dipping strata. (The celibate order of Benedictines - contrary to all evidence during Cuthbert's lifetime - attributed it to the displeasure of the saint at the possibility of women near his shrine.) Building was thus transferred to the confined space between the great west door of the cathedral and the edge of the gorge. (Its potentially perilous position was recognised in the early 15th century when four massive buttresses were erected to clamp it firmly to the rock. Inside, glass 'telltales' alert modern structural engineers to any movement.) The restricted site accounts for the unusual dimensions, its 23 metres width approaching that of the cathedral itself, but being only 15 metres long.

The late, or transitional, Romanesque design suggests knowledge of French Gothic architecture. Certainly, the chapel is not the cathedral writ large. While the latter is a massive show of strength, the chapel is an exercise in the delicate. The increased proportion of (15th century) window to wall admits a light which emphasises both a delicacy of sculptural form and purity of stone. Such quality of light, plus an entry which inevitably provides a view across a receding plane of chevroned arches springing from one slender cluster of piers to the next, encourages some to perceive a Moorish influence (Fig.3).

The arcaded hall consists of five aisles, each with four bays, with slender quatrefoil piers of twin sandstone and Purbeck limestone shafts. Close examination of abaci and bases, together with the piers against the west wall, show that originally the twin limestone shafts stood alone. The later sandstone pairs were presumably added for reasons of fashion, since a low wooden roof would hardly have presented any load-bearing problems. (The pock-marking on the limestone shafts resulted from the introduction of coke braziers in the 19th century, when the space was used by students of the newly-created university.)

A feature of the chapel is the remnants of its original 12th century wall paintings. They were not fully uncovered until the 1930s, when techniques for the removal of the ubiquitous whitewash had fortunately progressed beyond that of the Victorian era. On the jambs of the recess of the altar in the second bay from the north - the Lady altar - are full-length figures of a bishop and king, possibly St Cuthbert and St Oswald. On the spandrels of the arcade leading to the altar there are various depictions of crucifixion, martyrdom, Adam rising, along with a small group of Benedictine monks.

In the second bay from the south is the plain tomb chest, with Frosterley marble top and simple inscription, containing the remains of the Venerable Bede. (Up to the Reformation there had been an impressive shrine; when first brought to Durham, his remains had lain alongside Cuthbert in the feretory.) The central bay leads to the great west door, which was blocked with the building of the chapel, and more firmly so when Bishop Thomas Langley (bp 1406-37) placed his chantry tomb in front of the altar. Closure of the great west portal meant that a new main entrance to the cathedral had to be built – the present great north door and porch. To the door was attached the bronze sanctuary knocker which now greets every visitor, but which originally was grasped in desperation by fugitives. As a work of art it is considered beyond compare among Romanesque door rings. (The knocker seen today is actually a replica, the original having been placed in the treasury in the mid-1970s after restoration.)

The Chapel of Nine Altars was the second and last major addition to the church, being built as a spacious eastern transept to replace the original modest apsidal east end. Its dual function was to create a more impressive setting for the shrine of St Cuthbert and, as the name suggests, to provide altars for the saying of Mass by the monks. Begun in 1242, its completion took almost forty years – almost as long as it took to build the cathedral itself (Fig.4).

The dimensions are identical to those of Fountains Abbey transept, on which it was modelled by Richard of Farnham. Its height is emphasised by lowering the floor level below that of the choir – taking cognisance of the fall in ground and amount of unconsolidated material which thwarted earlier attempts to build a Lady Chapel – and by the slender lancet windows and fluted columns of Frosterley marble. (The dark limestone from Upper Weardale here appears on close inspection to be as much fossil as rock.)

The two outer bays, which are wider than the central one, have sexpartite vaulting in which their transverse ribs miss the centre of their bosses. Perhaps the dimensions of Fountains did not exactly transfer to Durham. The central crown of the central bay, however, is the focus of eight ribs. The width of this bay, of course, had to conform exactly to that of the Romanesque chancel to which it was joined. The joining of transept to choir was not a simple task, and not made any easier by the cracks which had appeared in the choir vaulting. Reconstruction involved building a link to the choir of a new, wider bay in the same style as that of the chapel. New vaulting was erected not only above the additional bay but also over the four existing bays, where the original had to be taken down. (Both vaulting ribs and transverse arches of the 13t[h] century work were enriched by the Durham trademark of chevron ornamentation.) Although the earliest vaulting was therefore lost, it gave a greater unity to the whole of the eastern part of the church.

Fig. 3. Galilee Chapel, looking south-east.

Fig. 4. Chapel of Nine Altars, looking north.

Behind the high altar there was now a platform projecting into, and elevated above, the floor of the Chapel of Nine Altars, on which the shrine of St Cuthbert was visible. The altars were along the east wall positioned in relation to the lancet windows. Above was a large rose window; the present window is a late 18th century restoration. On the north wall the geometrical Joseph window, with its double tracery, is unique in the north of England and the finest Gothic element in Durham. And, in common with the rest of the cathedral, the chapel was originally brightly painted. Minute traces can still be seen in the incisions on capitals and in blind arcading.

An Abbey Church

Architectural interest, and attraction, is not confined to the cathedral, since it was conceived and built as an abbey church. Nine years before the cathedral was begun, William of St Calais, himself a monk, had founded a Benedictine order at Durham. The celibate order replaced the more loosely organised Community of St Cuthbert. The monastery became one of the richest in the country, caring for the shrine of St Cuthbert and managing its vast estates. It also had nine outlying houses, stretching from Lindisfarne to Oxford and London.

At the Reformation, when the abbey was dissolved, the cathedral was stripped of its valuables and shrines, but nothing more. The explanation for the absence of further wanton destruction was a combination of the absence of irregularities or scandals, diplomacy of the bishop and prior and, perhaps, St Cuthbert himself. (The king's commissioners, on demanding that Cuthbert's coffin be opened, were taken aback, if not awe-struck, when the saint's body appeared 'uncorrupt'.) In due time, therefore, Durham was re-founded as the Cathedral Church of Christ and the Blessed Virgin Mary - Cuthbert being dropped - with a dean and twelve prebendaries, and all its estates handed back. The last prior was made dean and the prebendaries were chosen from former monks. As a result, Durham today has the most complete pre-Dissolution monastery in the country, both in its claustral buildings and in its outer courtyard. (It also has the country's largest archive of pre-Dissolution manuscripts.)

Two doors on the south wall of the nave give entry to the claustral buildings of the former monastery, which are conventionally arranged around a cloister. The Monks' Door, the westerly of the two, is a richly carved portal of foliage and beasts with strap iron tracery from 1130; the Prior's Door has an inner face of the same date, with an elaborate outer face with four elaborately carved, recessed orders from later in the 12th century. Between the doors evidence of the former scriptorium can be seen in the wall fixings marking the series of cubicles on this, the sunny side of the cloister. The cloister itself was then glazed, but this was removed when the present three-light tracery was inserted in the 1760s. Only the timber ceiling and bosses remain of the late 14th century construction.

On the east range the chief building is the Chapter House, the focal point of the monastery's daily administration. Erected 1133-40, it was controversially demolished in the late 18th century before being rebuilt a century later, close to the original design, and incorporating some surviving fragments, by Charles Hodgson Fowler. Ribbed vaulting, carved capitals and chevrons reveal the Durham pedigree. Beneath the floor are buried the Norman bishops.

Fig. 5. West Undercroft, looking north.

Fig. 6. Monks' Dormitory, looking north.

Fig. 7. Great Kitchen, vaulting ribs around central louvre.

Fig. 8. The Deanery, formerly the Prior's Lodging.

The west range contains two architectural highlights. On the ground floor is the mid-13th century Undercroft (Fig.5). Its series of short, circular piers supporting thirteen double bays with quadripartite vaulting have recently been revealed to great effect, to the extent that the modern experience exceeds anything that can possibly have be seen by the original medieval architect or its occupants. The glazed partitions between bookshop and restaurant have retained the unity of the space, which constitutes one of the most remarkable intact vaulted undercrofts in the country.

The dimensions of the undercroft, almost 200 x 40 feet, dictate those of the late 14th century Monks' Dormitory above (Fig.6). Attributed to master mason John de Middleton, it is the only intact monastic dormitory in the country. The monks' individual cubicles relate to the small, low windows, while above, tall Perpendicular windows light the whole interior. Its glory is the ceiling, where the baulk oak timbers spanning the width, with arched braces and wall posts, have the appearance of the upturned hull of a mighty wooden galleon. Its present function is as a Dean and Chapter Library and an exhibition space for pre-Conquest sculptures.

The south range contains the Refectory Library. As the name suggests, it was originally the monks' main dining room, but was converted in 1684 as the Dean and Chapter Library for early printed books. The present venerable, ordered appearance, with its 17th century bookcases, owes much to remodelling by Anthony Salvin in the 1850s.

Standing forward of the south range is the most precious claustral space, the Great Kitchen, designed and built by master mason, John Lewyn, 1366-74 (Fig.7). It is an octagonal building, with complex interlacing ribs of an eight-star vault unlike anything else in the country. It has been suggested that the inspiration came from the *maqsurah* of the Great Mosque in Cordoba. It is certainly a surprise to learn that the kitchen functioned, for the deanery, well into the 20th century. Today, as the Treasury, it houses the most precious relics of St Cuthbert (his coffin, pectoral cross, portable altar, embroidery and other early gifts) along with other historic treasures. Beyond the claustral buildings was the outer courtyard, the monastery's workshop, where a hive of activities were concentrated – granary, brewery, stables, guest house, infirmary, etc. Known today as The College, it is a tranquil area consisting of a large green enclosed by a harmonious composition of buildings, many outwardly Georgian, but all with medieval foundations and medieval fabric within. The Deanery, formerly the Prior's Lodging, is the clearest illustration, where the 13th century lower courses blend with the 18th century restyling with its large fenestration and tall chimney stacks. A late 20th century circular stairway to a first-floor door suitably completes the architectural patchwork (Fig.8). Hidden beneath is the prior's chapel, a 13th century structure recently restored as the Chapel of the Holy Cross. Adjoining the deanery to the north is Prior's Hall, a gracious room with 18th century wallpaper. Former deans, if not priors, lived in gracious surroundings.

On the south side of the green is a terrace of large prebendial – now canons' – houses, renovated in the 19th century. To the west some Tudor-Gothick treatment is evident, while on the lower, east side the more modest buildings probably derive from earlier monastic uses. The exception is the 16th century Gatehouse, with star vault and bosses beneath and St Helen's Chapel above. It connects with the Bailey.

Responses to 'the best building in the world'

It is to be expected that a structure called 'the best building' should have a string of observers who have eulogised on what they have seen. Here, perhaps pride of place might be be Nikolaus Pevsner, who became accepted as the 20th century's arbiter of taste of British architecture. Durham is described in several of his publications, not least the County Durham volume in his *Building of England* series. Bringing a comparative eye of a mid-European, he declared that:

> "Durham is one of the great experiences of Europe to the eyes of those who
> appreciate architecture, and to the minds of those who understand architecture." [9]

Pevsner's appreciation of Durham had actually begun nearly a quarter of a century before he made this assessment, while on his first visit to England in 1930. During a three-month tour travelling the length and breadth of the country he found English classical architecture undersized and feeble compared to mainland Europe – until he encountered Durham Cathedral. "It's the first thing that's made my heart race," he then wrote, "I'm just knocked over by it." [10]

The extensive traveller H.V. Morton, who visited Durham about the same time, underwent a not dissimilar experience:

> "Durham Cathedral: I shall have no emotion greater than this in any cathedral!
> This building is not magnificent: it is stupendous! It is the most wonderful
> Norman church I have seen, not excepting the great church of St Stephen at
> Caen. Its great nave is, with the exception of the hypostyle hall in the great
> Temple at Karnack in Egypt, the most awe-inspiring temple I have seen." [11]

In similar vein, Simon Jenkins considered the Norman cathedral to be "the most sensational man-made structure in Britain....I don't think anything of that period is its equal, not anywhere in the world." [12]

According to architectural historian, Alec Clifton-Taylor, the reaction of Morton and Jenkins would appear inescapable: "To step for the first time within Durham Cathedral must always be, for anyone in love with architecture, one of life's most thrilling experiences." [13]

The more restrained Samuel Johnson in the 18th century was still no less emphatic in his endorsement:

> "The Cathedral has a massiveness and solidity such as I have seen in no other
> place. It rather awes than pleases, as it strikes with a kind of gigantick dignity." [14]

Art historian Sir Roy Strong described the building as "the epitome in architecture of Blake's, 'And did those feet in ancient times....' " [15] (From the 17th century Durham had been described as the English Zion; with travelling clerics comparing its temple to that in Jerusalem.) Modern American writer, Bill Bryson, cast all comparison aside with his emphatic claim that it was "the best cathedral on planet Earth." [16]

The county's residents, once known as 'haliwerfok', O.E. for 'folk of the holy man', have always regarded their cathedral with pride. Articulation of their feeling may be lacking or, indeed, considered unnecessary - unless provoked. One such occasion occurred in the 1940s when a power station was proposed just downriver from the cathedral. Although supported by mine owners and union leaders, it drew opposing views in the correspondence of the local newspapers. Heartfelt was the following from the 'Miner' at the Blackhall Rocks Company:

"Most of us miners are neither chapel nor church goers, but we have a definite place in our hearts for the majestic loveliness of Durham cathedral. Durham is the miner's haven of peace, his Mecca…. We love to see the stately towers of Durham above the wooded Wear. I demand, in the interest of the Durham miners, whose sons and brothers have fought and fallen in both wars, that the erection of this power plant be forbidden to pollute the holy atmosphere of Durham." [17]

Durham cathedral is a highly visible structure, as the Blackhall miner remarked. It attracts attention long before the pilgrim or modern visitor has entered the building. Its dramatic setting permits all four elevations to be viewed from different positions, some near, some far. The standard two-volume work on Byzantine and Romanesque architecture by T.G. Jackson summarises the setting in the following terms:

The exterior of Durham, with its three massive towers, its enormous bulk, and its superb position on a rocky promontory round which the River Wear sweeps in a grand wooded defile, makes perhaps the most impressive picture of any cathedral in Europe." [18]

The view from the railway was declared by Ruskin to be one of the wonders of the world. [19] (Queen Victoria is said to have ordered the royal train to proceed slowly over the viaduct in order to appreciate the view.) Pevsner resorted to a painterly allusion in liking the view from Prebends' Bridge to a "vision of a Casper David Friedrich or a Schinkel." [20] Not surprisingly, a long line of painters – including Turner, Girtin and Cotman – have engaged with the scene, both from here and from many surrounding vantage points. [21] "England's most dramatic architectural composition" is how Jenkins assesses the scene in his recent survey of *England's 100 Best Views*. [22]

The contribution of the setting to the appreciation of the cathedral was emphasised by Clifton-Taylor in the strongest of terms: "At Durham nothing, absolutely and positively nothing, must ever be permitted to intrude upon the great views." [23] Four decades earlier, Thomas Sharp, who was to become president of both the Town Planning Institute and Institute of Landscape Architects, and who knew Durham intimately, was well aware of the challenge to his professions at Durham. In his words:

"Every cathedral city was designed to be a perpetual memorial to the history, continuity, struggles and, in a part anyway, the triumph of the Christian faith, on which European civilisation is largely founded. So heightened is this function at Durham by nature of the tremendous setting that the question of its mutilation becomes a matter of moment not merely to Durham or Britain but to Christendom." [24]

Sharp's words are an appropriate point on which to conclude this brief review in which a range of authorities confirm our subject to be an architectural innovation, aesthetic high and cultural benchmark. The next chapter will examine in detail the actual construction of the building.

2 The Building of the Cathedral: the Romanesque and early Gothic Fabric

The Romanesque cathedral of St Cuthbert at Durham, which was erected between 1093 and 1133, is one of the most celebrated edifices of its age not just in terms of English architecture but in a truly European sense. It is conceived on a monumental scale that rivalled works such as the imperial cathedral at Speyer (commenced c. 1030, nave groin vaulted and transept rib vaulted after c. 1083), the third abbey church at Cluny (commenced 1088), and a number of Anglo-Norman churches starting with the great Benedictine abbey church of St Albans (commenced 1077).[1] Durham is probably the earliest church in Europe to be vaulted throughout with rib vaults,[2] a motif that was to evolve as one of the hallmarks of Gothic architecture. Of course, the emphasis on mural mass and surface in Durham is entirely Romanesque, but Durham is often seen in a proto-Gothic context because the nave high rib vault has pointed transverse arches, and it has been argued that the quadrant arches across the galleries transfer the thrust of this vault to the aisle walls in a way that presages Gothic flying buttresses.[3] While a direct lineage between these motifs at Durham and their developed French Gothic counterparts is most unlikely, Durham may not have been without influence in the north of France and Normandy in the 12th century. More importantly, the rich articulation and delight in surface pattern in Durham cathedral set the standard for ecclesiastical architecture in Britain down to the 14th century. Durham created an aesthetic which fused Anglo-Saxon surface enrichment with the logical articulation of Norman design on a scale that spoke of the power of the new rulers of England. How this new aesthetic was devised is one of the questions we have to address by trying to ascertain the roles of the patron(s) and the master mason(s) in the design process. In so doing we examine the iconography of the cathedral, and consider where the first master mason might have been trained. There are no written records to assists in this quest; our assessment is made through a sleuth-like reading of the fabric in search of vital clues.

Documentation[4]

The monastic buildings begun by Bishop Walcher (1071-1080) are probably those in the east range to the south of the chapter house.[5] Between 1088 and 1091, during the exile of Bishop William of Saint-Calais (1081-1096), the monks built the refectory and probably the west side of the Deanery undercroft. The refectory undercroft does not correspond to the full length of the south cloister walk but was constructed in connection with the west wall of the first cloister which has been excavated in line with the third buttress from the south-west corner of the present cloister.[6] The scale of the present cloister was devised with the Anglo-Norman cathedral and therefore plans for the latter had not crystallised when the refectory was built. In 1092 Bishop William ordered the destruction of the Anglo-Saxon cathedral, and on 11 August 1093 he and Prior Turgot laid the foundation stones of a "fabric much larger and more noble, which he intended to erect." The monks built their own offices and "the bishop carried on the works of the church at his own expense."[7] After Bishop William's death in January 1096, the monks continued the work on the church and, according to Symeon's continuator, when Ranulf Flambard was appointed bishop in 1099 the building had advanced as far as the nave. This

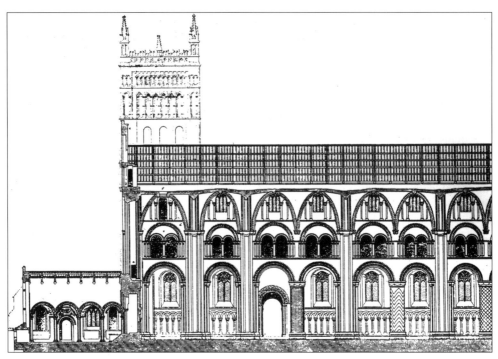

Fig. 9. Longtiudinal section of north side. (Plate I, Billings)

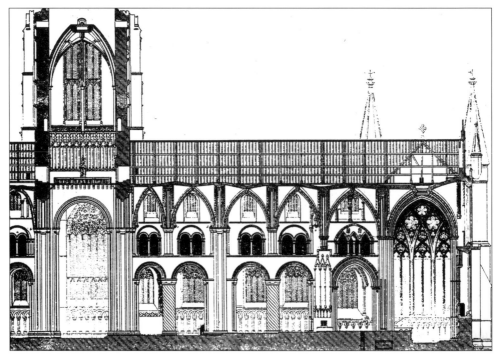

Fig. 10. Longtiudinal section of north side. (Plate II, Billings)

Fig. 11. Section of transept to tower and east (Billings)

probably means that no more than the lowest courses of the nave aisle walls had been built for it is unlikely that the full elevation of the choir, transepts and first bays of the nave could have been achieved in so short a time. During Flambard's episcopate (1099-1128) work progressed *modo intentius, modo remissus*. In 1104 the body of St Cuthbert was translated to its new resting place behind the high altar. At this time the eastern arm of the cathedral would have been complete except for the superstructure of the proposed eastern towers. Work was finished by 1128 with the exception of the nave high vault and the superstructure of the western towers. The nave high vault was erected by 1133 but the twin western towers were not finished until the late 12th or early 13th century.

The chapter house was constructed for Bishop Geoffrey Rufus (1133-1140). Bishop Hugh of le Puiset (1153-1195) commenced an extension at the east end of the cathedral but it collapsed and work was transferred to the west end where he built the Galilee Chapel. In 1242 work began on the Chapel of the Nine Altars to replace the main apse and the easternmost bays of the Romanesque aisles.[8]

Discussion

The replacement of the Anglo-Saxon cathedral with the present building conforms to standard practice after the Conquest, as at Canterbury (1070), Winchester (1079), York (1080), Worcester (1084), St Paul's London, or at Lincoln cathedral where the new Norman cathedral became the seat of the diocese moved from Dorchester (Oxon). At Winchester cathedral and great Benedictine abbey churches like St Albans, Ely and Bury St Edmunds, the new work was conceived on a scale far grander than pre-Conquest churches and one that revived the great early Christian basilicas of 4th-century Rome.[9] At Durham the length of the 1093 church was based on Old St Peter's in Rome, while the width of the choir and aisles combined at Durham is the same as the width of the nave of Old St Peter's, a fitting association for the new house of the shrine of St Cuthbert (Figs 9-12). These figures should be consulted throughout this chapter). Other elements of Romanesque Durham reflect other aspects of Old St Peter's. The spiral columns in the choir and transept arcades (Figs 17, 23, 24 & 31) are based on the baldacchino above the tomb of St Peter and the ribs of the vault recall the free-standing ribs of the baldacchino. They provide and iconographic link between St Cuthbert and St Peter.[10] It is also possible that the variety is the patterns of the main arcade columns at Durham ultimately reflect the variously coloured marble columns in the nave of Old St Peter's.[11] Roman association is also evident in the design of the west front of Durham cathedral with the giant enclosing arch on the nave façade and the lower similar forms on the aisle and gallery facades in the manner of the Arch of Constantine in Rome (312-15). It may be more than coincidence that the 28 flutes on the westernmost columns of the nave arcades match the number of flutes on the shaft of an Ionic column according to the 1st-century BC Roman architectural treatise, *De Architectura* written by Vitruvius.[12] One such extant manuscript of Vitruvius's text is British Library, Cotton Cleopatra D.i from which many copies descend, including a 12th-century copy from northern England, probably from Durham.[13]

The large scale of Durham cathedral is not new in post-Conquest England; St Albans abbey, Winchester Cathedral, Ely abbey (cathedral after 1106), Bury St Edmunds abbey, and St Paul's cathedral, London, were all created in this grand manner and in each case they housed an important local saint as at Durham. Like Durham, St Albans, Winchester and Ely had a four-bay eastern arm, an element unparalleled in churches in Normandy. Winchester cathedral may also provide the source for a number of motifs at Durham: the alternation of major compound and minor cylindrical piers in the main arcades, the interior aisle wall dado arcade; the stepped shafts of the aisle vault responds, and even a rudimentary forerunner of the shafts behind the columnar piers of the choir and transept arcades.[14] But Durham surpassed Winchester in decorative richness and articulation. The aisle dado arcades at Durham have moulded intersecting arches rather than the plain round-headed arches at Winchester (Fig. 15). The main arcade and gallery arches at Winchester are unmoulded (Fig. 14); those at Durham have angle roll and hollow mouldings and large soffit rolls that give plasticity to the arches (Figs 12, 13, 16, 17 & 24). Similarly, plain cylindrical piers at Winchester are given incised patterns at Durham, a translation into sculptured form of painted columns that can still be seen, for example, in the choir at Saint-Pierre at Chauvigny (Vienne). The same principle may have applied to the introduction of the rib in the vaults as a three-dimensional version of the painted groin of the type still extant in the presbytery aisles at St Albans abbey. Such a consideration compliments the iconographic association of the

Fig. 12. Nave, interior to east

Fig. 13. Durham Cathedral, nave interior looking north-east.

Fig. 14. Winchester Cathedral, north transept, interior to NNE (from John Britton, Cathedral Antiquities, Winchester (1836), pl. XII.

Fig. 15. Durham Cathedral, nave, south aisle: dado arcade and 13th-century decorative painting

Fig. 16. Choir, looking north west   Fig. 17. North choir aisle looking east

Fig. 18. Vault of fifth bay from crossing in nave south aisle.

rib with Old St Peter's baldacchino and also leads to the interpretation of Durham cathedral as a whole as the architectural shrine of St Cuthbert.[15] At Winchester the side shafts of the stepped aisle responds carry the groins of the vaults, at Durham the articulation of the aisle bays is given full plastic expression through the ribs and moulded transverse arches linking the stepped shafts behind the main arcade piers with those of the responds (Fig. 17). Thus each shaft and capital carries its own arched element in a logical manner that evolves from Winchester and ultimately from Norman works like William the Conqueror's abbey church of Saint-Etienne at Caen.

According to 19th-century rationalist theory, the rib served a structural purpose by reinforcing the groin of the vault through which it was believed the major forces were channelled to the corners of the bay.[16] However, the computer-assisted research of Robert Mark has demonstrated that the forces in rib and groin vaults are not first directed to the groin or rib and then to the corners of the bay, but that they funnel equally through the vault web towards the corners.[17] Whether the medieval architect knew this is another matter, but at least the continued use of groin vaults long after the introduction of the rib – especially in undercrofts where stability for the superstructure would be of paramount importance (e.g. in the dormitory undercroft at Kirkstall abbey) – suggest that the rib vault was not perceived as structurally superior to the groin vault.[18]

The rib did assist in the creation of truer diagonals within the vault, but the serpentine movement of some ribs at Durham indicates that the ribs were laid up with the vault web rather than being constructed in advance of the web (Fig. 18).[19] In other words, the Durham vaults were constructed in the same way as groin vaults. Complete wooden formwork was erected in each bay onto which the cut-stone ribs and rubble webbing were laid in mortar. When the whole was set, the formwork could be dismantled and moved to the next bay. The undertaking was a more complex version of the wooden centring for arches, some planks of which are still *in situ* in the enclosing arches of the nave galleries (Fig. 19). John Bilson tells us that in the nave high vault "between the tops of the ogives (diagonal ribs) and doubleaux (transverals) there is always a wide joint (of 2 inches or so) which received the boards of the centring on which the cells were built, and some fragments of oak boards were found in the course of repairs."[20] There are no such gaps in the choir and transept vaults, and throughout the church the ploughshared sections of the webs could only have been on full centring which also cradled the ribs.

Dado arcades are used on the exterior walls of the cathedral except in the cloister. Those on the north side were recut in the 1780s but the original form is still preserved on the south side of the choir (Fig 20). The apse of Saint-Nicholas at Caen provides a parallel for these arcades but the concept of the rich surface decoration recalls Anglo-Saxon practice, as on the tower of St Peter's, Barton-on-Humber (Lincolnshire) and the apse at Wing (Buckinghamshire).[21] While the intersecting arches of the internal dado arcades are not preserved in an Anglo-Saxon building, the motif can be traced back to the 8th century in the Canon tables of Insular manuscripts, as in the Canterbury Bible (London: British Library, Royal MS.1.E.VI).[22] The tall moulded plinths of the exterior walls and the main arcade piers find conceptual parallel in such pre-Conquest works as the chancel of St Wystan at Repton (Derbyshire) and the porticus entrance arch responds at Hadstock (Essex).[23] The high vault shafts of the gallery sills of the choir and transepts introduce articulation at first-storey level in the manner of the pilaster strips on the exterior of the chancel at

Fig. 19. Remains of wooden centring boards, nave south gallery

Fig. 20. South choir aisle exterior dado arcade

Fig. 21. Fragment of Romanesque vault web between Frosterley marble shaft and Gothic vault web, south side (DurhamChoirVaultdet)

Repton and upper external arcade of the chancel at St Laurence at Bradford-on-Avon (Wiltshire) where triple and quintuple shaft groups are created from single stone in the same way as the paired shafts of the Durham internal dado arcades. The crypt at Repton also provides a parallel for the spiral columns albeit on a far smaller scale than at Durham. Whether or not this last feature represents an element of Anglo-Saxon continuity after the Conquest, there can be no doubt that the ultimate iconographic reference is to St Peter's shrine in Rome.[24]

The three-storey elevation comprising main arcade with alternating major compound and minor cylindrical piers, gallery and clerestory may derive from Winchester cathedral choir, although the proportions of the tall main arcade and squat gallery at Durham are more closely presaged at St Albans.[25] Romanesque St Albans also had a high groin vault over the choir which provides a precedent for the vaulted presbytery at Durham.[26] It is also worth noting that the nave of the Mariakerk in Utrecht had a three-storey elevation with alternating major compound piers and minor columns – the latter with octagonal cushion capitals as at Durham – and a high rib vault. The Mariakerk was commenced in 1085 under imperial patronage which makes it a suitable candidate for emulation by an ambitious Anglo-Norman patron.[27] The Romanesque choir high vault was replaced with the present vault during the addition of the Chapel of the Nine Altars, but the form of the Romanesque vault can be reconstructed with some certainty. From the major piers the transverse and diagonal ribs of the Gothic vault spring from the three Romanesque shafts that rise from the ground (Figs 10 & 16). At gallery level these are flanked by Romanesque shafts surmounted by Gothic Frosterley marble shafts with stiff-leaf capitals which carry the wall arch of the vault. On the wall adjacent to each of the Frosterley shafts the scar of the original vault is clear. The scars arc up to the apex of the clerestory window but not beyond. This apparent asymmetry reflects the design of the Gothic vault rather than the Romanesque original. Above the minor piers the three Romanesque shafts set on the gallery sill carry the transverse and diagonal ribs of the Gothic vault. There are no Romanesque shafts to carry the Frosterley shafts and the Gothic wall arch, and therefore the Frosterley shafts are set on corbels. These shafts mask the traces of the Romanesque vault, but the erection of scaffolding in 1991 to clean the high vault afforded the opportunity for close examination behind the Frosterley shafts. In all cases the trace of the Romanesque vault was visible and in one case fragments of the Romanesque rubble web were still in place (Fig. 21). This evidence demonstrates that the trajectory of the Romanesque vault above the minor piers mirrored that above the major piers. These symmetrical lunettes accord with quadripartite rib vaults over single bays with transverse ribs above the minor piers and transverse arches above the central stepped triplet of the major piers. As in the aisles there is a one-to-one correspondence between the arched elements of the vaults and the shafts.[28]

The erection of a stone vault over the main span of the choir presented problems of stability. It has been suggested that the diaphragm arches behind the gallery piers provided abutment for the high vault (Fig. 22).[29] However, had the diaphragm arches been intended for a buttressing function then the stonework above them would have continued behind the springing of the high vault. As it does not, we must conclude that the diaphragm arches were used in connection with the roof structure over the gallery. The thrust of the high vault was therefore absorbed within the seven-foot thick wall. The pitch of the choir gallery roofs is not original because the sill of the

Fig. 22. South presbytery gallery, looking east

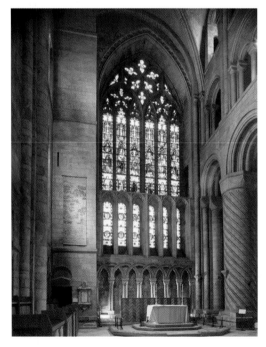

Fig. 23. North transept to north

Fig. 24. North transept from south nave gallery

Romanesque clerestory windows is about 18 inches below the top of the present roof.[30] A straight line between the Romanesque sills and the outer walls of the galleries would not clear the tops of the diaphragm arches. It is therefore likely that there were gablets over the projecting sections of the diaphragm arches.[31]

Against the outer walls of the galleries at the chord of the Romanesque aisle apses spiral staircases start upwards. It has been suggested that these would have risen up as turrets (Fig. 22).[32] As such they would not have given access to any other part of the building, in contrast to the turrets at Peterborough abbey (now cathedral) which surmount staircases on the inner angles of the apse chord and provide a link between the gallery and clerestory. Therefore, it seems more likely that these Durham staircases were connected with towers over the square enclosed apses of the Romanesque church. This reading is supported by fragments of Romanesque ashlar on the guttural wall above the apse chord diaphragm arches, and on the north side by a break in the coursing of the stonework on the corresponding clerestory buttress. This break is explained by the removal of the west wall of the tower when the 13th-century extension of the choir was built.[33] Confirmation that the staircases in the responds of the apse-chord arches of the Durham galleries were connected with towers is found in the south nave gallery at Peterborough abbey (c. 1150). Against the outer wall of the gallery, opposite the penultimate pier of the Romanesque nave at Peterborough, a spiral stair starts up in the manner of those at Durham. The Peterborough stair is built against the east side of the respond, rather than within the respond as at Durham, but otherwise the parallel is exact; and most importantly the Peterborough staircase was constructed in connection with the planned western towers of the Romanesque fabric. The main arcade and gallery piers at this point are bigger than those to the east, and they are accompanied by broader transverse arches than in the other bays in the aisles.[34] Also, the removal of the stonework above the transverse arch at Peterborough has left a mark like that on the walls above the transverse arches of the apse chord at Durham.[35] Eastern towers were used in the Romanesque fabric of Hereford cathedral and possibly at St Albans abbey and Winchester Cathedral. Such towers appeared before 942 at St Maximin at Trier, yet it may well be that the Durham scheme of towers flanking the apses may have been adapted from the stair towers that flank the apse of the imperial cathedral of Speyer and ultimately those at Old St Peter's, Rome.

The Durham transepts present a number of anomalies. Four highly articulated bays on the east contrast with three relatively plain bays on the west. Massive stair turrets project from the outer western angles both on the exterior and into the interior space (Figs 11, 23, 24, 31 & 33). The arches of the eastern bays diminish in scale from the crossing outwards, and the details of the clerestories and the ribs of the high vaults are different north and south. How are these anomalies to be explained?

The projecting stair turrets house spiral stairs 67 inches wide. This width is most unusual in the context of major Anglo-Norman churches in which staircases are generally about three-feet wide. One important exception is the main staircase in Remigius's westblock at Lincoln Cathedral which is 58 inches wide. The Lincoln westblock was conceived as a fortified structure, and it is in castle keeps that parallels for the Durham stairs are found. The closest in form to Durham – especially to the stair turrets in the western towers – is Castle Hedingham (Essex) which is

60 inches wide and is set in a turret which projects into the interior space.[36] This analogue, along with the multi-towered plan and the massively thick walls, suggests that the cathedral was designed in concert with the fortifications of the peninsula.[37]

The four bays on the east side of each transept provide three separate chapels in the eastern aisles and access to the choir aisles. The scale of the arch next the crossing was determined by the choir aisle, while each transept arm was generated in plan by doubling the square of the crossing. The first square extends from the centre of the crossing pier to the centre of the major pier of the east arcade and its west wall respond; the second from the centre of the major crossing pier to the outer face of the stair turret.[38] It seems strange that the outer face of the turret was aligned with the outer line of the square, unless it was conditioned by the length of the south transept in relation to the Anglo-Saxon church. Be that as it may, the chosen geometry results in the second bay on the east side occupying the space left between the arch to the choir aisle and the major transept pier, while the two outer bays are reduced in scale because the outward projection of the stair turret and the thickness of the transept terminal wall are set within the square planning module. With this reduction in space it is not surprising that the length of the major pier in each transept is significantly less than in the presbytery: the use of a presbytery-scaled pier would have left insufficient room to entrance to the chapels. A concomitant of this pared-down length is the reduction of the vault shafts above the minor piers from three in the choir to two in the transepts (Figs 12, 20). This is reflected in the form of the high vault in which two diagonal ribs spring from the shafts between bays one and two with no transversal. The two outer bays are covered with a single quadripartite vault and therefore the shafts between the third and fourth bays on the east simply continue up the wall to the web of the vault, like the shaft on the west wall of the main crypt at Christchurch priory (Hampshire).[39] Such apparent lack of logic in the articulation may suggest that the transept high vaults were not conceived at the outset.[40] There is indeed evidence in the south arm for the erection of a wooden roof before the introduction of the present vault, but in the north transept the evidence speaks unequivocally of the intention to vault from the first. The formeret (wall arch) immediately below the vault web on the north wall is a motif which is only ever constructed in connection with a vault. The shaft in the north-east angle of the north transept that carries the formeret of the high vault rises from the floor and courses with the Romanesque stonework of the main arcade and gallery throughout its length (Fig 23). That the capital and abacus here range with the capital and abacus carrying the high-vault rib, and the adjacent stones in the spandrel of the gallery arch, and the shafts of the wall arch and the high-vault rib range with the adjacent gallery shafts and capitals, can only mean that the high vault is integral with the initial plan (Figs. 25 - 26). This is confirmed by the shaft carrying the south-east diagonal rib of the high vault in the north transept which is set on the gallery sill next to the north-east crossing pier in exactly the same way as the analogous shafts at the west end of the choir where they carried the diagonals of the Romanesque high vault (Figs 27 - 29). And, just as in the choir, this transept shaft, complete with its capital and abacus, courses perfectly with the adjacent stonework. The masonry to either side of the ribs in the spandrel between gallery bays 1 and 2 of the north transept is set at different levels; this could only occur if the ribs were built with the wall (Fig. 30). Finally, the clerestory passages behind the vault springers are just 7 feet 6 inches in height in order to provide as mass of masonry behind the springing of the high vault to act as abutment.

Fig. 25. North transept, north-east corner, detail   Fig. 26. Detail of Fig. 25
of gallery arch and springers of
formeret (wall arch) and high-vault rib

The high-vault ribs spring from the west wall of the north transept not from capitals atop sill-set shafts, but from corbels. The reason for their use is not hard to find. The first storey of the west wall has a triforium passage rather than a gallery as on the east side. Had the front plane of the triforium been 13 inches in the manner of the gallery, the passage would have been reduced to just 12 inches in width and thereby rendered it useless as a means of access from the north-west staircase to the north nave gallery.[41]

The evidence in the south transept does not speak with the singularity of intention to vault witnessed in the north transept. On the east side of the south transept the arrangement up to the springing of the gallery arches is the same as in the north. Above this there are clear indications that the vault was an insertion. The capital next the crossing that carries the diagonal rib of the high vault is set higher than the crossing capitals, whilst the vault capitals between the first and second bays are clumsily placed (Figs 31 & 32). The south-easternmost shaft, intended for the wall arch of the terminal wall as in the north transept, carries the south-east rib of the high vault, whilst the shaft planned for this job rises to the webbing of the vault (Fig. 33 & 34). Most importantly, in both the east and west clerestories there are former openings that were blocked to facilitate the construction of the high vault.[42] The openings were created in connection with a wood roof which preceded the present high vault. In the wood-roofed scheme the clerestory

Fig. 27. North respond of east crossing arch, west respond of north choir gallery and high vault shaft

Fig. 28. North transept, coursing of SE high-vault capital and shaft with east respond of north crossing arch

Fig. 29. Crossing, detail of north-east shafts and capitals

Fig. 30. Springer of high vault over bays 1 and 2 in east gallery, north transept

Fig. 31. Bays 1 and 2 of east side of south
transept

Fig. 32. South crossing arch capitals and capital
and springer of south transept high vault

Fig. 33. Bays 3 and 4 of east side of south
transept

Fig. 34. Bay 4 of east side of south transept,
detail of shafts and vault springer

Fig. 35. West crossing arch, detail from south-west

Fig. 36. Nave, north aisle, looking east

passage was 11 feet in height, as opposed to 7 feet 6 inches in the north transept, because there was no need of the abutment afforded by the masonry above the lower passage. The ribs of the high vault are ornamented with chevron as in the nave rather than the roll and flanking hollows in the north transept which go with the choir aisles.

If the north transept was built as planned with the high vault, while the wood roof constructed over the south transept represented a change in plan, the implication is that the north transept was built before the south. This is unusual for a church with monastic buildings on the south side. Be that as it may, delay in completing the south transept may have occurred if it was built over part of one of the Anglo-Saxon churches which remained until after the translation of the relics of St Cuthbert into the new church in 1104.[43] With this in mind, it is possible that the south column of the main arcade of the south transept which has chevron incisions, in contrast to spirals in the other transept and choir main arcade columns, is possibly intended as a marker of a former church.[44]

Unlike the choir and transepts, the nave was not initially planned for a high vault. The front plane of the gallery is not set back from the main arcade, as in the choir and the east elevation of the transepts, and the north-east and south-east ribs of the nave high vault commandeer shafts that were originally intended to carry the outer order of the western crossing arch (Figs 13 & 35).

Fig. 37. Quadrant arches, before addition of two inner orders, nave south gallery (after Billings)

The wood-roofed scheme was soon abandoned, however, and by the time the eastern clerestory bays were constructed the plan for the high vault was in hand. The stepped design of the inner plane of the clerestory follows the north transept, while the use of head corbels to carry the high vault ribs is continued from the west wall of the north transept. The chevron that adorns the high rib vaults was introduced in the second major campaign of construction. Before discussing this campaign, certain differences must be noticed between the nave, on the one hand, and the choir and transepts, on the other, that were planned in the first great campaign. The nave aisles are wider than the choir aisles, the result of erecting the inner plane of the nave aisle wall in line with the outer plane of the aisle wall in the choir. The minor piers of the nave arcade are 8-foot cylinders rather than 7-foot cylinders in the choir with attached shafts towards the aisle to carry the transverse arches and diagonal ribs of the aisle vault (Fig. 36). The nave aisle responds opposite the columnar piers are also demi-cylinders. In the first great campaign of construction two bays of the main arcade with the corresponding aisle vaults and one bay of the gallery were built on each side. Thus the lozenge decoration on the first pair of columnar piers in the nave, rather than the spirals in the choir and transepts, was determined in phase 1, a continuation of the decorative variety introduced in the chevron column in the south transept main arcade. With the resumption of work in phase 2, chevron is introduced in the main arcade, gallery and clerestory arches, the doorways, as well as the vault ribs and the second pair of columnar piers. Whether

35

Fig. 38. South west tower, detail to north-east

or not this is the earliest chevron in England, it sets the standard for the shrine-like enrichment of churches in Britain through the remainder of the 12th century. Further diversity comes with the flutes on the third pair of columnar piers. The inner faces of the north and south doorways are also encrusted with sculpture; there are foliated and figured cushion capitals, and figured medallions on the hood mould, and on the shafts of the north doorway.

As in the presbytery, the erection of the high vault over the nave has led to discussion of abutment and in particular to the interpretation of the quadrant arches over the nave galleries as proto-flying buttresses (Fig. 37). Billings suggested that the 'Norman flying buttresses' were erected 'to counteract some extraordinary pressure tending to thrust the walls outward'.[45] Billings's interpretation was followed by many architectural historians, while others have argued that the quadrant arches did not function as supports for the high vault.[46] Stephen Gardner's detailed study of the arches would seem to have put the matter to rest and his views were accepted by Eric Fernie and the present author, and most emphatically by Paul Crossley.[47] Yet, as recently as 2005, Lindy Grant referred to the Durham flyers.[48] Be that as it may, just as the diaphragm arches in the choir galleries were built in connection with roof, so were the nave gallery quadrant arches.[49] A series of transverse gables covered the nave galleries traces of which are seen in Billings's engraving of the south elevation before its restoration in 1850, and are still visible in certain bays on the north side.

There has been much ado about the introduction of pointed transverse arches in the nave high vault, another feature that is supposed to presage Gothic (Fig. 12). It is true that the pointed form does avoid the stilting evident in the round-headed transverse arches in the transept high vaults, but it does little to transfer the trust of the vault more closely to the vertical of the supporting walls and therefore seems to present little in the way of structural advance. Moreover, the mural mass at Durham is quintessentially Romanesque.

The core of the north doorway to the cathedral remains from the Romanesque period but it has undergone considerable reworking since its construction in the 1120s.[50] The present frame of the doorway is the result of the "improvements" of the 1780s. Pre-restoration engravings show that there was a two-story Gothic porch, the foundations of which have been excavated. This took the place of a Romanesque porch, the evidence for which is a flight of stairs leading to the first storey of the porch from the north nave gallery, and two small windows, now blocked, on the inner face of the wall above the doorway. The original was probably like the north porch at Kelso Abbey.

The twin-towered façade of Durham develops from Edward the Confessor's Westminster abbey, Christchurch cathedral at Canterbury and St Augustine's abbey at Canterbury.[51] In all these examples the ground floor of the towers communicated with the western bay of the nave through full-height main arcade arches, and is similarly open to the aisles. This openness presages the developed French Gothic *façade harmonique* as at Reims cathedral. The inclusion of towers involved a modification of the design principles elsewhere in the nave. The alternating system of compound and columnar piers is abandoned to provide massive piers strong enough to support towers. The tower bays are larger than the aisle bays and therefore the capital carrying the vault rib on each tower pier is set lower than the arcade capitals to avoid an unduly segmental trajectory of the rib (Fig. 38).

Our appreciation of the Romanesque west front is diminished by the addition of the Galilee Chapel and the great west window, and by the late 18th-century chiseling back of the wall surface. But even if the detail cannot be trusted, at least the main lines of the design are clear. Pilaster buttresses express the internal division of nave and aisles, while the lowest three windows on the tower fronts correspond to aisle, gallery and clerestory. The two lower storeys are framed by giant arches that originally rose uninterrupted through the two storeys, and the enclosing arch of the central section of the façade is still extant.

The chapter house was erected between 1133 and 1140 in the usual place to the south of the south transept from which it is separated by the barrel-vaulted slype. The walls of both the chapter house and slype have (restored) intersecting blind arcades in which the dosserets and shafts are created from monoliths, a motif formerly used in the crypt of Lastingham priory and subsequently in the chapter house at Rievaulx abbey.[52] The doorway has a richly chevroned arch and inhabited capitals on the inside by the same sculptors as the north and south doorways of the church. The modern vault incorporates the original rib design with chevron flanking the earliest keeled roll in England.

The roles of the patron and master mason in the design

The design of the cathedral would have been established through dialogue between the patron - initially Bishop William of St Calais probably in consultation with a building committee - and the master mason. Concepts of scale, the number and location of towers, and the inclusion of high vaults would have originated with the patron. Thus parallels of size and iconography with Old St Peter's, Rome, would have been Bishop William's. His sense of rivalry with the new "shrine churches" at St Albans, Winchester, Bury St Edmunds, Ely and St Paul's Cathedral, London, would also have influenced the overall scale of the church as well as the four-bay choir, the alternation of the main arcade piers, multiplication of towers and turrets, richness of decoration, and the high vaults. He would have been aware of the compatibility of the design with the castle and the fortification of the peninsula. He would have been instrumental in initiating the Anglo-Saxon references as appropriate for the new architectural shrine of St Cuthbert, although his input on individual motifs, versus that of the master mason, is likely to remain a matter of debate. If the intersecting dado arcades were inspired by the canon tables of pre-Conquest manuscripts then such reference to the art of church treasures was more likely driven by the patron than the mason. To this we may add reference to the Franks Casket (London, British Museum), a whale-bone box which was probably made in the north of England in the first half of the 8th century, a time and location close enough to be associated with St Cuthbert.[53] In the scenes of the Adoration of the Magi paired shafts like those in the Durham dado arcades, stepped plinths and roll mouldings in the arch. The latter feature multiplies to four rolls in the arch in the scene of the Sack of Jerusalem by the Emperor Titus. In the arch that represents Egil the Archer's home there is chevron ornament and the columns have bold interlace decoration. The parallels are not exact but when considered as a group, and contrasted with the post-Conquest great churches like Winchester cathedral, they indicate an Anglo-Saxon aesthetic appropriate for the architectural shrine of St Cuthbert. Mention should also be made of the possibility of Islamic sources for intersecting arcades and chevron, as in the Cristo de la Luz, Toledo (990).[54] Obviously, such a source does not have the immediate connection with St Cuthbert provided by the Anglo-Saxon parallels for these motifs but the taste for the exotic is a factor to be considered. It may also be more than coincidence that the motif of divergent high vault ribs that spring from corbels on the west walls of the Durham transepts and above the minor piers in the nave also appears in the vaults of the Cristo de la Luz.

Specific details would have come from the master mason. The setting of the moulded bases of the presbytery arcade piers and aisle responds on huge rectangular plinths with a single chamfered step is allied to the former crossing piers and nave arcade responds at Lastingham priory (1078-85) where the high groin vault in the presbytery is an important precursor, albeit rebuilt, of the Durham vaults.[55] Cushion capitals are also used at Lastingham and in the 1070s work in the west range of Jarrow abbey, while scalloped capitals, like those in the aisle dado arcades at Durham, were used in Archbishop Thomas of Bayeux's (1070-1100) York Minster. The double-splay windows in the middle storey of the axial tower at Jarrow (after 1083) presage the original choir clerestory windows and the lowest window in the north transept stair turret at Durham.[56]

Soffit rolls and other roll mouldings in major arches are presaged on the west crossing arch

Fig. 39. Nave arcade column detail

Fig. 40. Nave arcade column detail

at Blyth priory (commenced 1088). The exterior articulation of the east clerestory of the south transepts speaks of an English, rather than a Norman, tradition. The string course that runs between the windows and continues as the hood of the windows is set one course above the abaci of the capitals of the window. This detail is paralleled in the north doorway of Laughton-en-le-Morthen (Yorkshire). Something analogous also features in the belfry arches in the Saxo-Norman west towers in the North East at Billingham, Bywell St Andrew, Monkwearmouth and Ovingham. The roll-and-hollow moulding at the angle of the Durham south transept clerestory windows is framed by a large expanse of plain archivolt on the front of the arch. This contrasts with Norman arches in the moulded part of the arch forms its own order. Yet there is a pre-Conquest analogue for the expanse of stone between the angle moulding and the hood mould on the west doorway at Earls Barton (Northamptonshire). Moreover, if the restored archivolts of these Durham windows truly reflect the original masonry then the varied large size of the individual stones belongs to the tradition of Anglo-Saxon construction rather than Norman masoncraft with its smaller radiating voussoirs. Further reflection of pre-Conquest masonry practice is seen in the paired shafts of the internal dado arcades which are created from single stones in the manner of the triple and quintuple shaft groups in the blind arcade of the chancel at St Laurence, Bradford-on-Avon (Wiltshire).

The patterned columns of the Durham main arcades find small-scale precedent in the crypts of St Peter's, Utrecht, and St Lebuinus, Deventer, both of the mid 11th century, and the dormitory of Christ Church, Canterbury, of c. 1080. The latter have been associated with an Anglo-Saxon tradition and the same may be argued for the spiral and chevroned shafts in the belfry of the west tower at Appleton-le-Street (Yorkshire). In this connection, the lozenge pattern on the easternmost nave arcade columns at Durham may be associated with a similar design on one of the tenth-century hogsback tombs in Gosforth church (Cumbria).[57] A precise parallel for this design at Durham is found on some painted plaster from the Romanesque fabric of St Mary's abbey, York, preserved in the Yorkshire Museum.[58] St Mary's abbey, York, was founded by King William II, in 1088, and it is likely that the painted decoration, as well as other motifs from this Yorkshire monastic church influenced the work at Durham. Construction of the patterned columns at Durham is remarkable for the precise planning and execution of the stonework, which was first noticed by R.A. Cordingley and later brought into the mainstream literature by Jean Bony.[59] In these columns the size of each stone is uniform and was carved in the workshop before the stone was carefully set to produce the pattern on the cylinder (Figs 39 & 40).

Galilee Chapel[60]

The Galilee was constructed at the west end of the cathedral by Bishop le Puiset after an abortive attempt to build an extension at the east end (refer Fig.3). It has five aisles, each of four bays with round-headed arcades carried on slender quatrefoil piers with coursed limestone and dark marble shafts. The initial plan was for the paired marble shafts to stand alone, but the limestone shafts were soon added, thereby creating an image of greater stability. In the main, the additional capitals and bases are carefully fitted to the originals, but in certain cases the new capitals have not been provided with abaci. The rich chevroned arches follow the design principle of the main church but otherwise the mouldings are more delicate than the earlier work, not least the

Fig. 41. Lindisfarne Priory, nave south arcade

Fig. 42. Selby Abbey, nave south arcade

keeled rolls in the soffits and the waterleaf capitals. The emphasis on mural mass in the main church is here replaced with a sense of spaciousness which displays knowledge of developments in French Gothic architecture. This was probably transmitted via Archbishop Roger of Pont l'Évêque's new choir at York Minster, as rebuilt after 1154 and perhaps in the contemporary work in the cloister at Bridlington priory.[61] Affiliated work is seen in the castle chapel at Newcastle, in Bishop Puiset's hall (now chapel) in the Bishop's Palace at Bishop Auckland, in the north nave arcade at Hornby (N. Yorkshire), and elsewhere.

Chapel of the Nine Altars[62]

In 1235 Hugh Northwold, Bishop of Ely (1229-1252), granted an indulgence which offered thirty days remission to those contributing to the fabric fund of Durham where the vault over St Cuthbert's tomb was in imminent danger of collapse. At this time Bishop Richard Poore of Durham was planning to extend a new work at the east end of the church to provide a safer and more fitting place for Cuthbert. Work was started in 1242 and was completed about 1280 (refer Fig.4). The general association of an eastern transept with a shrine is allied to Beverley Minster and Worcester cathedral (1224-1232), but Durham was modelled directly on the Nine Altars at Fountains abbey (commenced c. 1203-8). The free-standing columns at the entrance to the transept arms are abandoned at Durham. However, other aspects of the plan are copied exactly, and this created alignment problems with the east and west vault responds, which contributed to the uncomfortable junctions between the transverse arches and the diagonal ribs in the bays next to the centre of the chapel.

The walls of the Chapel of the Nine Altars are seven-feet thick as in the Romanesque fabric, and the richness of articulation and decoration follow similar principles even though the detail is different. The dado arcade in the Nine Altars is much deeper and its spandrels are excavated with elongated quatrefoils. Above this the wall dissolves into a passage with tall lancet windows, and this is surmounted by a clerestory passage. The elevation follows closely the eastern extension at Tynemouth priory which was erected to give a more magnificent setting for the shrine of St Oswin. The wall of the north front of the Nine Altars above the dado arcade is filled with a huge six-light bar-tracery window.[63] The mass of the responds is denied by the strong verticals of grouped limestone and marble shafts. Prolific stiff-leaf foliage sprouts from the capitals, and dog-tooth and other ornament encrust arches and vault ribs the way chevron embroidered these elements in the second phase of the Romanesque building. The rich decoration plus the use of marble shafts allies the Nine Altars Chapel with the shrine setting at Worcester and Ely cathedrals.

Influence and Affiliations of Romanesque Durham

Romanesque Durham influenced the design of buildings from Orkney to northern France and Normandy.[64] Lindisfarne Priory, a daughter house of Durham, was rib vaulted throughout, and was probably conceived as a cenotaph to St Cuthbert (Fig. 41). The alternation of compound piers and incised decorated columns and corresponding compound and demi-cylindrical responds reflect Durham nave. The nave-vault shafts set on the gallery sill follow the choir and east side of the transepts at Durham, while the corbelled high vault in the choir, crossing and transepts at Lindisfarne follow Durham transept west walls. The arch and rib mouldings are Durham-inspired, and the west porch with upper-storey watching room probably reflects the north porch at Durham.[65]

The nave of Selby abbey has alternating major and minor piers and the first column of the south arcade has incised lozenge decoration (Fig. 42).[66] The vaults in the two eastern bays of the south nave aisle have soffit rolls on the ribs like those in the choir and transept aisles at Durham, and at the back of the incised column they are carried on stepped shafts in the manner of the choir and transept aisles. Whether or not the design similarities between Selby and Durham represent a direct connection between the two buildings or a reflection of the lost source at St Mary's abbey, York, is a moot point. The three western bays of the north nave arcade at Kirkby Lonsdale

(Cumbria) are usually compared with the nave of Durham cathedral.[67] Formally there are many similarities, including the alternation of columns with a compound pier, the incised lozenge decoration of the columns, the octagonal cushion capital of the eastern column, and the plinth mouldings.[68] Kirkby Lonsdale was given to St Mary's Abbey, York, by Ivo de Taillebois, between 1090 and 1097.[69] At Workington (Cumbria) the soffit roll flanked by wide hollow mouldings on the inner order of the tower arch is the same as in the choir and transept arcades at Durham, and the projection of the stair turret in the north-east corner of the tower recalls the transept stair turrets at Durham. Workington also belonged to St Mary's abbey, York, and therefore the Durham parallels may also reflect York influence.[70]

The Thwing (Yorkshire) font has incised lozenges in the manner of the Durham nave piers, and the same type of font occurs at St Oswald, Flamborough (Yorkshire), where the inner order of the chancel arch has two rolls separated by an angle fillet. At St John Baptist, Carnaby (Yorkshire), the drum-shaped font is covered with lozenge decoration filled by chevrons and rosettes. At All Saints, Nafferton (Yorkshire), the drum shaped font has crude diapers with various infillings, and a top band of loops.

At All Saints, Kilham (Yorkshire), the profile of the plinth of the buttresses of the south nave wall is the same as for the transept and nave arcade piers at Durham cathedral and Jumièges abbey and parish church. Kilham uses ashlar construction for the nave and in the gable of the south doorway there is rich *opus reticulatum* including a vertical chevron pattern and lozenges. The doorway has seven orders each carved with various chevrons. Capital 4L of the south doorway has three scallops on each face and incised outlines, and a swollen angle scallop of a type found in the choir aisle dado arcade at Durham. At the time of Domesday Kilham was owned by the king and between 1100 and 1107 Henry I gave it to York Minster.[71] At All Saints, North Dalton (Yorkshire), fragments of lozenge incised masonry is reused in the south wall of the nave.

At St Andrew, Bolam (Northumberland), there are some incised decorated stones reset above the jambs of the former sanctuary arch which are probably inspired by the Durham incised columns.

In the nave arcades of Norwich cathedral and Waltham abbey columns with incised spiral decoration like the Durham choir and transept arcades probably served as liturgical markers for nave altars within an alternating system of supports.[72] Incised geometric decoration like that at Durham also occurs in the crypt piers of Archbishop Roger of Pont l'Évêque's York Minster (after 1154), and formerly in the nave piers of the Cluniac priory at Lenton (Nottinghamshire).[73]

Richard Fawcett has observed that King David of Scotland (1084-1153) looked chiefly to Durham Cathedral for his masons.[74] The chevron on the chancel arch of Edinburgh castle chapel and the east processional doorway at Holyrood abbey depends on Durham. At Dunfermline abbey incised columnar piers are again used as liturgical markers, while all the arch mouldings, the rib vaults and the intersecting dado arcades of the nave aisle, and certain details of the sculpture of the doorways are Durham-inspired.[75] At Kirkwall cathedral, the rib-vaulted choir aisles, arch mouldings, intersecting dado arcades in the transepts and nave aisles, and the stair turrets that jut into the outer western angles of the transepts, all betray a detailed knowledge of Durham.[76] Durham also influences the external blind arcades and grotesque corbels for rib vaults at Dalmeny (Lothian) and Leuchars (Fife). On a different level, the vast scale of St Andrews cathedral-priory, the location of the shrine of the patron saint, the transept plan with eastern aisles, and the rich arcaded decoration in the choir and transepts all reflect Durham.[77]

The rib-vaulted chancels at Warkworth, Heddon-on-the-Wall, and formerly in free-standing chapel at Bamburgh Castle (Northumberland), have vault shafts set on a string course at the level of the window sill in the manner of the gallery sill-set shafts in the choir and transepts at Durham. Various details at Corbridge, Seaton Delaval and Old Bewick, Ponteland (Northumberland), and Heighington, Kirk Merrington (rebuilt 1850),[78] Lanchester (Co. Durham), and chevron fragments at St James-the-Less, Durham, all speak of Durham cathedral-trained masons. Similarly, the form of the chevron of the gatehouse arch at Alnwick castle (Northumberland) takes its form from Durham, while the head corbels that carry the transverse arch of the barrel vault in the gatehouse of Prudhoe castle (Northumberland) are inspired by the high vault corbels in the Durham nave and transepts.

The one grotesque head corbel remaining from the high vault added to the nave of Lincoln cathedral by Bishop Alexander (1123-48) suggests the influence of Durham, and a similar head in the north-west angle of Bishop Alexander's choir of Stow (Lincolnshire) belongs to the same family. More generally, the rib vaults at Winchester cathedral added after the 1107 fall of the crossing tower, and those at Peterborough abbey, commenced in 1117/8, may have been inspired conceptually by Durham.[79]

Later in the 12th century, variants on the spiral decoration of the choir and transept main arcade columns appear in the nave of the nearby church of St Cuthbert at Pittington, in which there are also remains of contemporary wall painting of the life of St Cuthbert stylistically related to Bishop le Puiset's wall painting at Durham cathedral. Greater variety in decorated columns occurs in the choir of the former collegiate church at Orford (Suffolk).

The degree to which Durham influenced rib vaulting in Normandy is difficult to determine, not least because the high rib vault in the presbytery of the abbey church at Lessay was completed before the burial of Eudes de Capel there in 1098 and may even have been commenced before Durham.[80] Durham may lie behind details like the grotesque corbels carrying the ribs at Tollevast (Manche) and the choir aisle groins in the former abbey church at Saint-Gabriel, but the influence does not appear to have been direct.[81] Later, the nave of Saint-Pierre at Lisieux has a recessed gallery with sill-set shafts interpreted from Durham.[82]

Certain details in the westblock of Abbot Suger's Saint-Denis suggest Durham contact, including the lower setting of capitals taking diagonal ribs, and rich articulation of piers, responds and arches. The gables over single bays of the galleries of the early Gothic cathedral at Arras recall the former gables over the nave galleries at Durham,[83] and later *facades harmonques*, like Reims cathedral, ultimately reflect Durham.

Perhaps the most lingering aspect of Durham's influence concerns the concept of a rich decorative aesthetic with the multiplication of shafts on piers and mouldings in arches, and a wealth of applied ornament. The indulgence in linear pattern and surface encrustation continued into the early Gothic with the choir of Canterbury Cathedral (1175-84) and Glastonbury abbey Lady Chapel (1184-6/9), throughout the Early English of Lincoln cathedral (1192-1280), and Ely cathedral presbytery (1234-52), to the richly textures walls of Decorated Exeter cathedral (c. 1270-1390), and Ely cathedral Lady Chapel (c. 1321-69).[84]

Acknowledgement

I should like to thank The Dean and Chapter of Durham for permission to have total access to the cathedral without which this study would not have been possible. In the early 1990s, Mr Owen Rees, Head Verger, and Mr Reg Wright, Assistant verger, were models of helpfulness during my many visits. Mr Ian Curry, architect to the fabric of Durham cathedral, accompanied over the building on many occasions, kindly gave permission to examine the choir high vault from scaffolding in 1991, and freely shared his wealth of knowledge on the fabric. In 2013, Philip Davies, Chapter Clerk, graciously facilitated my access to the upper parts of the cathedral. I have benefitted from discussion with Dr Eric Cambridge, Ms. Linda Denesiuk, Mr Stuart Harrison, Professor M.F. Hearn, Professor Lawrence Hoey, Dr Hugh McCague, and, most particularly, with Professor Eric Fernie. My visits to Durham in 2013 was generously funded by the Social Sciences and Humanities Research Council of Canada. I am most grateful to Dr Douglas Pocock for the opportunity to publish my revised views in this essay.

3 The Interior Decoration of the Cathedral

'…wch cover was all gilded over and of eyther side was painted fower lively Images curious to ye beholders and on the East End was painted the picture of or Savio^r sittinge on a Rainebowe to geive Judgm^t very lively to ye behoulders and on the West end of it^t was the picture of or Lady & Savio^r on her knee…'

The above description of the cover over St Cuthbert's shrine is only one of hundreds of references to paintings, carvings and other decoration in the *Rites of Durham*.[1] Although dating from the 1590s, the *Rites* describes the cathedral and monastery as they were just before the Reformation. Almost certainly by a former monk of Durham, it provides a unique record of how a cathedral looked and functioned in the late Middle Ages: not as the relatively empty building we see today but crowded with altars and other furnishings; not as an isolated church but as an integral part of one of the greatest monasteries in Europe. Therefore, in this chapter although the focus will be on surviving painted decoration in the cathedral, it will also include the equally interesting but little known paintings in the monastic buildings, and try to set all these – albeit superficially – within the context of the many other furnishings that contributed to the 'decoration' of both cathedral and monastery.

One all-pervading theme in the decoration was St Cuthbert himself, whose shrine was the major focus of pilgrimage in northern England. In the late Middle Ages, as we know from the *Rites* and other sources, he was depicted in more than eighteen windows in the cloister and elsewhere; much of this glass was given by Bishop Langley (1406-37), and must have resembled the surviving St Cuthbert window also given by him to York Minster. But only a few images of the saint now survive at Durham, most notably the celebrated late 12th-century wall painting in the Galilee Chapel (Fig. 43), where he is accompanied by St Oswald (the Northumbrian royal martyr whose head was kept in Cuthbert's shrine). Of similar date is a highly important but virtually unknown wall painting concealed by panelling in what was originally the monks' refectory, and is now the Chapter Library. Discovered in 1962, this painting on the east wall has been severely keyed for a later layer of plaster, but at the south end a number of large standing figures can still be made out including a bishop and a king (Fig. 44), while at the other end a 'recumbent figure of a man, with head thrown back and arms raised' is recorded. Since it was a well-established tradition to represent a monastery's patron or patron saint in the refectory, these paintings must almost certainly show St Cuthbert.[2] They would have formed a fitting backdrop to the great feast of St Cuthbert held every year on the day of his death.

Although the *Rites* affords a marvellous impression of the appearance of the cathedral in the later Middle Ages, it is less useful for understanding the early decoration of a building whose impact now results chiefly from its enormously powerful Romanesque architecture. Much the most striking decorative effect in the Romanesque building is created by the lozenges, chevrons and spirals carved deeply into the piers. Carved decoration of this type – at least on such an enormous scale – seems to be a Durham innovation, and subsequently reappears in other buildings dependent on or influenced by it, as mentioned in chapter 2. The spirally grooved piers, consistently associated with important features such as altars, appear to be 'meaningful' in that sense, and depend on a tradition extending back to the Early Christian period.[3] Although this architectural carving may originally have been coloured, there is now apparently no trace of *any* painting in the cathedral to be associated with the original building. Doubtless some existed, including perhaps figure-subjects in important locations, but in general it seems that the decoration of early Romanesque buildings was often as austere as their architecture – at Winchester Cathedral, for example, examination of the 11th-century transepts has revealed that the main or perhaps only decorative effect was achieved by the prominent white pointing of the masonry itself.[4] There are, however, surviving continental examples of Romanesque buildings with elaborately painted piers, and very likely the carved decoration at Durham represents a more expensive version of similar painted decoration once existing in England. At Exeter, late 11th-century columns from St Nicholas' Priory were found to be painted with spirals, and lozenge and scale patterns; and a fragment of painting of similar date from St Mary's Abbey, York, also has a lozenge design very like that occurring in Durham.

In the late Romanesque and early Gothic additions to the cathedral, a polychromatic effect was achieved partly by the very effective contrast of the buff-coloured sandstone masonry with limestone polished to resemble marble. The Galilee Chapel at the west end, dating from c.1175-80, shows an exceptionally early use of Purbeck marble in the shafts (paired with freestone shafts) in the arcades, while the Nine Altars Chapel at the east end, begun in the 1240s, has a splendid array of shafts in the local Frosterley marble, in which a curious 'splodgy' effect is created by the large coral fossils. This chapel also retains some of the earliest surviving architectural polychromy in the cathedral with remains of red, blue and black on the arcade enclosing the altars, and of further colouring in a few of the quatrefoils above. Also from the mid 13th century are simple, but exquisitely executed, painted decorative motifs, reflecting the same restrained taste as the grisaille glass used contemporaneously in the cathedral's windows.[5] In the prior's chapel (now part of the Deanery), dating from between 1244 and 1254, such decoration still survives on a jamb of one of the lancet windows (Fig. 45) and on the jamb and soffit of the north doorway.

The survival of similar decoration in the cathedral itself indicates that in the 13th century the Romanesque building – as at Ely, Peterborough, and elsewhere – was given at least a partial 'face-life' through painted ornament. In the south transept there are remains of foliate scrollwork with flowers and a trefoil-ended stalk on the wall of the northernmost altar, and similar ornament survives on an adjacent Romanesque capital. But the most extensive survival of the 13th-century decoration overlaying the original Romanesque architecture is in the blind arcading in one bay of the nave south aisle: here one section has been reproduced in modern repainting, clearly showing the scheme of masonry pattern (lining imitating the joints between blocks of masonry), scrollwork and stencilled rosettes, while traces of delicate foliate sprays survive in some of the spandrels above (see Fig. 46). Fragments of this scheme also survive in the vaulting of the aisle – foliate decoration on a rib and arch soffit – and probably also of the same date is the design of repated four-petalled motifs (somewhat reminiscent in appearance of carved dogtooth) discovered in 1990 on the soffit of the south-east doorway. Most interestingly, the bold black chevrons painted on one of the aisle responds deliberately imitate – over a century later – the carved chevrons of the pier opposite. Nor was this type of imitation confined to Durham itself; at nearby Finchale Priory, the 13th-century choir piers were painted with chevrons and other geometric designs in a clear

Fig. 43. Nave south aisle: dado arcade and 13th-century decorative painting, including chevrons on the respond.

Fig. 44. Refectory, east wall: detail of 12th-century paintings, showing a king and other figures. (Crown Copyright).

Fig. 45. Galilee Chapel, northern altar recess: St. Cuthbert, c. 1180. (Crown Copyright).

Fig. 46. Prior's Chapel (now Deanery): Adoration of the Child. c. 1475-80 (Crown Copyright)

reference to the mother house – in what indeed could be termed the Durham 'house style'.[6]

While at least some of the architectural polychromy of the cathedral can be pieced together from surviving fragments, another type of painted decoration – of the many stone and wooden screens dividing the internal spaces of the cathedral – is more difficult to reconstruct. The Rites describes a screen across the east end of the nave, with 'the whole stories & passion of our Lord wroughte in stone most curiously & most finely gilte, & also above… was all the storie and pictures of the XII apostles… very fynelie gilte'. Two panels from this screen, datable to c.1155, still survive, one showing the Transfiguration and the other Christ appearing to Mary Magdalene and to the two Marys after the Resurrection, but nothing remains of 'the most goodly & famous Roode [crucifix]' that was set above the screen. In general, pitifully little is known about roods and their screens at this period, but some light on the Durham arrangement may be shed by paintings elsewhere that were originally associated with roods. At Kempley (Glos.), the nave east wall paintings of c.1130 undoubtedly once framed a sculptured rood, and include a representation of the Marys at the Sepulchre (symbolising the Resurrection) on the south side. At Ickleton (Cambs.), approximately contemporary paintings on the nave north wall comprise, like the Durham screen, scenes of the apostles (all martyrdom subjects) and of Christ's Passion, and

Fig. 47. Prior's Chapel (now Deanery): 13th century foliate ornament on window jamb, based on Cufic Lettering.

Fig. 48. Gailee Chapel: damaged scene of the Coronation of the Virgin above the northern altar recess, with figure of St. Cuthbert blessing to the right (c. 1300)

end with the Carrying of the Cross; the Crucifixion itself was probably represented in the form of a carved rood at the crossing, followed by post-Crucifixion scenes painted on the south wall.[7] It seems very likely, therefore, that the iconography of the Durham screen was by no means untypical, that the apostle scenes were mostly martyrdom subjects, and that the Christological series began with Passion scenes to the north of and 'preceding' the crucifix, and ended with post-Resurrection scenes 'following' it to the south. Various other screens in the cathedral are described in the *Rites* such as the choir screen with carved images of kings and bishops, and such smaller examples as the painted wooden screens dividing the altars in the Nine Altars Chapel. Here, there were doubtless screens between the altars originally, but from the description of the painting as 'branches & flowers and other imagerye most finely… pictured and guilted', it would seem that this decoration, at least, was of later medieval date.

It was, of course, partly to provide more altars at which the monks could celebrate that the Nine Altars Chapel was constructed. In addition to the normal daily round of worship, some of the most important liturgical ceremonies of the year were associated with Easter. From Easter

Fig. 49. Galilee Chapel: Crucifixition (with Adam below rising from his grave and holding a chalice), flanked by the martydoms of SS. Peter and Paul (c. 1300)

Fig. 50. Galilee Chapel: Martydom of St. Paul (c. 1300)

Fig. 51. Tomb of Bishop Thomas Hatfield (d. 1381): angel at the foot of the bishop's effigy

Fig. 52. Prior's Chapel now Deanery: detail of the Resurrection (c. 1475-80)

to Ascension, a huge bronze paschal candlestick was erected before the high altar; almost certainly of 12th-century date, and so enormous that it could only be lit through a hole in the vault, its decoration included flying dragons, flowers, crystals and armed horsemen as well as the evangelists. Normally kept disassembled in the north choir aisle, it was polished each year by children from the almshouses before being erected.[8] Another object with a specific use at Easter was a curious image of the Virgin, Our Lady of Bolton, to whom an altar in the south transept was dedicated. This sculpture is described in the *Rites* as

> 'a m[r]veylous lyvelye and bewtifull Image of the picture of our Ladie… whiche picture was maide to open w[th] gym[mers] [or two leaves] from her breaste downdward. And w[th] in [ye] said image was wrowghte and pictured teh Image of our saviour, m[ar]veylouse fynlie gilted houlydinge vppe his hands, and holding betwixt his hands a fair & large crucifix of Christ, all of gold'.

At Easter, this crucifix was taken out and displayed in the choir, and then every monk 'did crepe uvot it that was in ye churche as the Daye', before its symbolic burial in a temporary sepulchre. It must have been a rare example in England of a *Schreinmaddona*, a type first introduced c.1300 and of which examples still exist in Germany.[9]

Our Lady of Bolton was just one of scores of images of the Virgin in the medieval cathedral. For instance, she occupied the central position of the Neville Screen, erected in 1376-9 largely at the cost of John Lord Neville. This screen, still a magnificent backdrop to the high altar, was prefabricated in London and sent up in boxes via Newcastle; originally its central images were alabaster figures of the Virgin flanked by SS. Cuthbert and Oswald, 'all richly gilded'.[10] That this late medieval composition may well have reflected an earlier arrangement at the east end is suggested by the late 12th-century paintings in the Galilee Chapel. Here, the jambs of the northern altar recess are painted with life-size figures of St Cuthbert (Fig. 43) and St Oswald, and the back wall within imitation draperies but with a vertical strip in the centre left plain probably to accommodate a carved image. Evidence that this altar was dedicated to the Virgin is provided by two references: a charter of the 1180s, referring to an altar of St Mary in the Galilee (though without stating its position); and the Rites reference to an altar of Our Lady on the north side of the chapel. Originally, therefore, it may well have contained a central sculptured image of the Virgin, while additional confirmation of the dedication is provided by a painting of c.1300 on the wall directly above. Although only the lower half survives, the painting clearly showed the Coronation of the Virgin within a circular frame, once again with a figure of St Cuthbert to the right (Fig. 47).[11] This altar of the Virgin would have been particularly suited to the devotions of women, who were not allowed access to the main body of the church, and such a use is perfectly captured in the 1180s charter, in its reference to a husband and son offering a gift to St Cuthbert's altar in the church, but the wife to Mary's altar in the Galilee.

On the south wall of this aisle in the Galilee is the only extensive series of painted figure-subjects in the cathedral. They belong to the same scheme as the Coronation of the Virgin on the east wall, and the combination of subjects is reminiscent of the 12th-century rood screen: a central Crucifixion flanked by scenes of the twelve apostles (the three westernmost are now lost), all set within a painted arcade of trefoil-headed arches. The Crucifixion, alone of the series, extends into the spandrel of the arcade below; here Adam is depicted rising from his grave and holding Christ's blood in a chalice, symbolising man's redemption through God's grace (Fig. 48). The representations of the apostles include one of Doubting Thomas, oddly showing the saint with a rich fur lining to his cloak, but most are wonderfully vigorous martyrdom scenes. St. John is boiled in oil, St. Peter crucified upside down, and St. Paul beheaded – the executioner here grasping the long hair at the back of the saint's otherwise bald head (Fig. 49)! The black flesh of figures such as the executioner wielding an enormous ladle in the St. John scene is a particularly striking feature. It might be thought to signify evil were it not that Adam and the Virgin, for example, show the same characteristic. In fact, these black areas were scientifically examined in 1991, and found to be lead white pigment that had subsequently altered; this is a widespread phenomenon in medieval wall paintings, occurring most famously in those by Cimabue in the upper church at Assisi.[12] No doubt the same explanation applied to the 12th-century refectory paintings, which, when found in the 1960s, were thought to be unfinished because of their black faces.

The 14th and 15th centuries saw, as in other great churches, a veritable invasion of the cathedral by magnificent tombs and chantry chapels. All lavishly decorated, and typically including elaborate displays of heraldry – reflecting the increased secularity of the age – these monuments profoundly affected the interior appearance of the cathedral. A particularly important chantry was that of the Neville family in the south aisle of the nave, from which the splendid if battered tomb of John Lord Neville (d.1388) and his wife still survives. But the finest monuments at Durham were to the bishops themselves, previously more modestly interred in the chapter house. Among the first to receive such a memorial was Bishop Louis de Beaumont (d.1333). His enormous brass, stretching across the floor in front of the high altar and characteristically including figures of his ancestors 'in theire coate armour', was the largest and finest of its date in England, though only the indent now survives. Even more ostentatious was the chantry of Bishop Thomas Langley (d.1437) located in the Galilee, and completely blocking the west doorway of the nave. The most prominent tomb of all, however, was that of Bishop Thomas Hatfield (d.1381) which still survives on the south side of the choir. In this amazing structure, built during Hatfield's lifetime, the tomb is combined with a throne above; the modern repainting and gilding, though distressingly gaudy, nevertheless afford some impression of the splendour of the original polychromy. Fine, though fragmentary, paintings still remain on the interior walls of the tomb: angels as heraldic supporters at the feet of the alabaster effigy (Fig. 50), and, at its head angels taking Hatfield's soul to heaven in a napkin. Above the latter painting was a depiction of the Majesty displaying his wounds, now mostly lost but known from an 18th-century drawing.

The priors too indulged in lavish patronage in the late Middle Ages, providing, for instance, almost all the major stained glass of this period in the cathedral. Indeed, much the finest late medieval wall paintings still existing in the north of England were executed for one of their number, probably Richard Bell (1464-78) or Robert Ebchester (1478-84). Absurdly little-known, these paintings decorate the north wall of the prior's chapel (now the entrance hall to the Deanery) and were discovered behind panelling only in 1974. Four scenes are set within a painted architectural arcade, each illustrating a verse from a hymn to the Virgin contained in the border below. The first scene, the Annunciation, is badly damaged, but the seated figure of the Virgin with a lectern behind her can still be made out. Next is the Nativity (Pl. 51), in the late medieval form of the Adoration of the Child, deriving from the revelations of the 14th-century visionary, St Bridget of Sweden. The Christ Child is shown on the ground, lying on a cushion and surrounded by a glory, while the Virgin, Joseph and the midwife kneel in adoration. The Resurrection then follows, the Virgin kneeling on a tasselled cushion and worshipping Christ as he steps from the tomb, with two guards in elaborate plate armour to the left (Fig. 52). Although little is visible of the fourth scene, enough remains of the inscription to identify it as the Ascension, and probably there was a final scene of the Virgin's own Assumption. Although major alterations to the prior's quarters are documented under John Wessington (1416-46), the style of the paintings and the evidence of the armour and costume – particularly the fashionable dress of the midwife, with her tight-fitting bodice, flat collar and loosely slung girdle – suggest a somewhat late date of c.1475-80. The only really comparable wall paintings from this period in England are the famous series in Eton College Chapel showing miracles of the Virgin, and likewise heavily influenced in style and iconography by contemporary Netherlandish painting. Whereas the Eton scenes are much more complex compositionally and show an interest in spatial setting almost entirely absent at Durham, their essentially grisaille palette is very subdued in contrast to the gorgeously coloured Durham paintings. Although the sophisticated technique at Durham has yet to be fully analysed, the blue pigment, for instance, has been identified as the vegetable dye indigo, applied in no fewer than three different ways. [14] No more fitting climax to the medieval decoration at Durham could be found than these superb paintings, venerating the Virgin like so many works before them

4 Continuity and Change: Masters, Surveyors and Architects to Fabric of the Cathedral

The Norman cathedral, rising from the rock of the peninsula, has foundations which gave the church an unmatched structural stability, while its superstructure was so well engineered that only one major change was needed when its eastern end was extended in the 13th century. However, any building which remains in continuing and constant use is not a static monument, but a living structure subject to continuous adaptation and change. It is on the nature of the subsequent upkeep of the original Norman building, and on the authors of adaptation and change that this chapter will focus.

The early Centuries

The names of the Norman Master Masons at Durham are not known, but a few names begin to emerge from the middle of the 12th century, when we have the names of two of the designers employed by Bishop Hugh of Le Puiset – Richard de Wolveston, who was probably responsible for the Galilee Chapel starting about 1170,[1] and followed by William the Engineer (both referred to as Ingeniator).

The most important alterations to the Norman building came in the middle of the 13th century with the addition to the east end of an eastern transept, or Chapel of Nine Altars, in place of the Norman apse, mainly to provide ample space round St Cuthbert's tomb for pilgrims. The high-vault of the quire was renewed at the same time, so that an extremely subtle harmony between the Romanesque and Early English work was achieved. This Chapel of Nine Altars is a marvellous space, and such was its enrichment in mouldings and sculpture that it took as long to build as the whole Romanesque cathedral had done – forty years. Richard of Farnham was responsible for the new Chapel; Thomas Moyses (c.1240) was also associated with the works, probably as mason.

In the 14th and 15th centuries we have the names of a handful of prominent Masters. Roger the Mason was working on the Gatehouse Chapel in 1339 and probably inserted the Great West Window into the cathedral in 1341. John Lewyn was most important in the latter half of the 14th century as master mason to the bishop, as well as working on some of the royal castles, for the Nevilles at Raby, and for John of Gaunt. He was designer of the new Priory Kitchen in 1368; with its interlacing ribs to the octagonal vault one is tempted to wonder what link there might have been with ideas from Spain, where John of Gaunt was claiming the Kingdom of Castile. Lewyn probably started the new cloisters at the end of the 14th century and may have designed the Hatfield monument (1362-71), but was not responsible for the new tomb-base for St Cuthbert's Shrine or the Neville Screen (1171-80), both of which were made in London workshops in the most up-to-date Court style, and may have been designed by Henry Yeveley. The masons John de Middleton in 1398 and Peter Dryng in 1401 contracted for the reconstruction of the Great Dormitory,[2] with Ellis Harpour as carpenter, and also John Dinsdale as mason. Peter Dryng undertook the tomb and chantry of Bishop Shirlaw in 1402, while Thomas Hyndeley completed the cloisters between 1416 and 1430.

John Bell, Senior, worked on the infirmary from 1418-29 and the Prior's Lodging 1428-32. With William Chaumere, he inserted four new traceried windows into the quire in 1438; and two years later placed tracery in one of the nave windows. This, of course, was part of the process when all the main windows of the cathedral were either enlarged or had tracery inserted. In 1429 the central tower and its steeple suffered lightning damage and a fire; it was repaired 1430-37 was John Bell, Senior. Of this earlier crossing tower we know very little other than it may have been carried up at much the same time as the western towers, and that there was decorative metalwork in its steeple. After a second fire in 1459 the tower was rebuilt 1465-75 to the designs of Thomas Barton from York. The belfry stage was completed by John Bell, Junior, starting in 1483 and continuing until towards the end of the century. The belfry had been prepared with internal squinch arches for large corner pinnacles such as most late medieval towers would have had, but at Durham these were never completed. We shall see how our18[th] and 19th century architects sought to remedy this omission.

The 16th century brought the Dissolution of the Benedictine Monastery, but it was relatively gentle. The King's Commissioners had taken down the shrine of St Cuthbert, but the throne, Neville Screen and Castel Clock survived, the last-named moved from the crossing into the south transept. In the 1540s Chapter minutes mention the purchase of incense, and setting up the great Pascal for Maunday Thursday, and it was not until the 1570s under a puritanical dean that the pascal was destroyed and much else besides.

After the Dissolution, the Dean and Chapter records begin to make occasional references to repairing the 'leades' of the cathedral roofs between 1541-96, and also to work on re-hanging the bells in the central tower, but no names of craftsmen are mentioned.. Nor is the maker of the new marble high altar installed for Dean Hunt in 1626. The bells were recast "to a solemme tune of six notes" in 1631 by Umfrye Keyne [3] (to be recast by Christopher Hodson in 1693). In these early years of the 17th century there was a positive interest in Durham of restoring furnishings and services to something like they were before the destructions of Elizabeth's reign, but the Civil War was to be disastrous for the cathedral. All the internal wooden furnishings which had survived the Reformation were damaged, firstly by the invading Scottish troops in 1640, and then finally destroyed by the Scottish prisoners from Dunbar in 1650. The lead-covered timber spires or great broaches' of the western towers (Fig.53) also were taken down.

Restorations, 1660-1774

> The first meeting of the Chapter after the Restoration, on 3rd November 1660, recorded:
> "That Whereas the fabrics of the church and Chapter House is Exceeding Ruinous, the Leads much decayed, the Windows almost totally broken, and noe seats in the Quire, but such as have been made since his Majesties happy Restoration........Hospitalities, Residences, etc. are impossible to observe for the present by reason of Raines of the Deanery and Prebendaryes homes and want of furniture and other accommodation......[4]

Two days later John Cosin was elected bishop, and the next day the Chapter recorded:

Fig. 53. North Front before 1660, with lead-covered spires on west towers

Fig. 54. North front, 1754, "with minerets" pencilled in by Thomas Wright, 1770

"That some workmen of several professions be employed to View the Delapidations of the Church, Chapter House, College, School House, and all other buildings either to the Church in generall or to the Deane and prebendaries in particular, And that thereupon Care be taken for Repairacions, with all convenient speed….. and that for the present 10 trees be cutt down and brought to the College to be seasoned this winter for making Stalls and seats in the Quire next Spring." [5]

So it would seem that the chapter had planned the new stalls before Bishop Cosin's enthronement, though as completed they were very much in the style associated with him, richly mixing Gothic canopy-work with Renaissance and Jacobean elements. It was a style that ad already been established before the Civil war by Cosin and his fellow prebendaries in some of the parish churches of County Durham. John Clement may have been the designer or carver in charge of the work in the cathedral, [6] and so convincingly medieval is the tabernacle-work, one suspects that fragments of the originals may have survived to provide models for the new work: rather more Renaissance detailing appears in the lofty font canopy, and the choir screen was to be almost Baroque. John Cosin always had the keenest interest in the pre-Reformation survivals in Durham, and both his pre-Civil War and Post-Restoration works in and around Durham should be regarded as Gothic Survival rather than early Gothic Revival. In July 1661 the Dean and Chapter reordered a "fair double organ" [7] from George Dallam of the parish of St Andrew by th Wardrobe, London, and this was in use by the end of 1662. The splendid organ which eventually surmounted the choir screen was built 1683-86 by (Father) Bernard Smith. [8]

John Sudbury had been dean since 1662, and before his death in 1684 he had arranged for the old frater or Petty Canons Hall to be rebuilt as a library. With its fine bookcases and reading desks in the style of a college library, it still stands much as he intended. The deanery itself was said to be "in great decay" but was partly rebuilt on its northern side by the early 1690s. John Bowes may have been Supervisor of Works or Clericus Operum to the Chapter at this time, and his is the first recorded name in the Chapter Minutes of what was to be a continuous line of men overseeing the work on the fabric of the cathedral. (The actual title Clericus Operum does not appear in Minutes until 1720. From this time on in the 18th century the Clericus Operium was to be constantly engaged on works about the cathedral and College.) Repaving of the quire in marble was started in 1729, and paving the rest of the cathedral in stone continued until 1738. The cloisters were repaired 1763-69 with Mr Hogg as Clericus Operum, and it must have been at this time that whatever survived of the 15th century tracery of the cloisters was replaced by the present plain intersecting and uncusped tracery, which looks far from authentic. The basic 15th century piers and buttresses of the cloisters survive, though repaired in the 19th and 20th centuries.

Revival and Improvements, 1774 to 1827

The last quarter of the 18th century saw the advent of Early Gothic Revival works, marking the second phase of cathedral restorations. The 18th century also saw a series of topographical illustrations. There are several engravings showing the appearance of the north front prior to 1770; the western towers without parapets, just as they had been left after the removal of the great broaches; the two-storeyed Gothic north porch, with the royal arms of Elizabeth l set above the Norman portal; the angle turrets of the north transept with pyramidal roofs; and the north-east turret of the Nine Altars lopped off at eaves level. It was Forster and Mynde's 1754 view of the north front which Thomas Wight used in 1770 to depict proposed new pinnacles, or "Minerets" as he called them, on the west towers, central tower, and north end of the Nine Altars (Fig.54). Already in 1770, then, some enlightened people were thinking the cathedral exterior needed embellishment.

By this time it must have been becoming evident to the Dean and Chapter that the fabric of the cathedral needed attention, and at Dean William Digby's first Great Chapter on 20th November 1777, it was "Agreed that Mr Wooler be Employed to Survey the Church, and to make an Estimate of the Expenses of Repairing and Beautifying it." [9] It would seem the Chapter was as much concerned with improving the appearance of the cathedral as repairing its fabric. John Wooler, a Newcastle surveyor and engineer, was assisted by a Mr Gibbons and George Nicholson. (The latter, an architect and mason who lived in Bow Lane in the shadow of the cathedral, had recently designed the new Prebends' Bridge, built 1772-75 to replace the previous one swept away in the Great Flood of 17th November 1771.) Wooler seems to have reported verbally to members of the Chapter as the survey proceeded. His report was written at Durham, and set pout repairs needed to the fabric of the church, most of which came to be carried out over the succeeding years. The four corner turrets and the eastern buttresses of the Chapel of the Nine Altars were reported as being in a bad way, and also the gable and turrets of the north transept. A rent or crack had been discovered along the south side of the nave vault, though he thought it was not recent. He drew attention to the very poor state of all the external masonry, and proposed that it be chipped or pared away to a depth of one, two or three inches in order to remove weathered and decayed surfaces. Work was needed on the stonework of many of the windows, on the parapets and buttresses of the central tower, and on the north porch where the upper part had pulled away from the main structure. Wooler recommended that the western towers be properly finished with pierced parapets, and that they and the central tower should have "ragged pinnacles" to relieve their massive appearance. He finished by calculating that it would take eight years for a team of forty men to complete the work at a cost of £9,000.

Thus, we have in this 1777 Report the essence of the works on the fabric of the cathedral during the next twenty years – the destruction of the ancient north porch: the chiselling away and resurfacing of the masonry of the east, north and west fronts of the church; the reconstruction of the north gables and upper parts of the northern turrets to the Nine Altars Chapel and North Transept; and the addition of pinnacles to the central and western towers, the first of several schemes for 'finishing' the top of the central tower, which never had received the pinnacles intended by its medieval designers.

The Chapter records do not indicate in which order the works were carried out, but expenditure was authorised on the repairs from 1778 onwards. However, in February 1779 Wooler presented his 'memorial' or specification for taking down and rebuilding the north gable of the Nine Altars, including the construction of the present octagonal north-west and north-east stone spires of the chapel. This work must have proceeded immediately, to be followed in later years by the remainder of the north side of the cathedral. The Chapter paid Wooler 30 guineas in July 1782 "for his trouble in viewing and reporting the state of the Church." The amount of the payment helps to confirm the view that Wooler had been brought in as a consultant, but that the day-to-day organisation and supervision of the repairs was left to the Clericus Operum, and to Nicholson. (Records suggest that Nicholson was acting both as 'College Architect' and 'Clerk of Works' to the chapter by 1777.)

Wooler had proposed to the Chapter in the 1777 rep[ort that Nicholson be employed to measure and draw proper plans and elevations of the cathedral, so as to assist in "designing and depicting" the proposed beautification of the church. None of the original drawings have survived, although the first edition of William Hutchinson's History of Durham (1787) gives two plates showing the north and east elevations, prior to the repairs being started, the north elevation being inscribed "Durham Abbey from a Measurement by G. Nicholson, Arct." The east front is shown with its north-east turret still truncated, lead-covered spires to the south-east and south-west turrets, and flanking rose window, an arrangement of the large central buttress and their niches with statues very different from that which now exist. More important, two original pen-and-wash drawings by Nicholson survive in the library of the Society of Antiquities in London giving the west front and north front "as proposed." They show the 'ragged pinnacles' on the central tower and western towers as proposed in Wooler's report, and also show the north porch virtually in its present form, as are the north turrets to the Nine Altars and north transept.

Hutchinson, writing in 1787, draws particular attention to the recent chiselling of the north front, and to the north porch having been "rebuilt and highly ornamental". [10] Thus, the porch had been reconstructed in its present form by 1787, and almost certainly under the direction of Nicholson. All the chiselling and re-dressing of the lower parts of the east front will have continued under Nicholson until his death in 1793. He was succeeded by William Morpeth. That the Chapter appointed him as architect rather than clerk of works is significant, for it is clear that he soon established himself as a dominant character in the College. He remained in office until 1814.

In February 1794 Durham also received a new dean, James Cornwallis, later Earl Cornwallis, who was already Bishop of Lichfield and Coventry, and on 26th September 1794 the Dean and Chapter "Agreed that Mr James Wyatt be wrote to, to come down to inspect the repairs to the Cathedral and to Give a Plan on the future Repairs and Improvements." [11] Wyatt (1747-1813) had earlier been called in by Bishop Shute Barrington to remodel the gatehouse of Durham Castle, and at this time was at the height of his career. Whatever his detractors might have said, he was the most fashionable architect in the country, the undisputed master of the Gothic style. Wyatt in due course presented his report and proposals, his set of drawings dated September 1795 being preserved in the Chapter Library. If he made a written report, it has not survived, but his intentions are clear from the drawings.

Wyatt's drawings quite distinctly indicate that the Galilee Chapel was to be removed, not for bringing a carriage drive round the church as popularly supposed, but to allow the great west door to be re-opened. It was to be given a new outer porch, or rather the recently re-cased Nicholson north porch was to be moved to the west door, and the northern entrance eliminated.

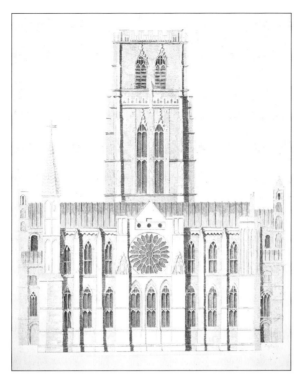

Fig. 55a. East front of Chapel of Nine Altars, 1777, drawn by George Nicholson

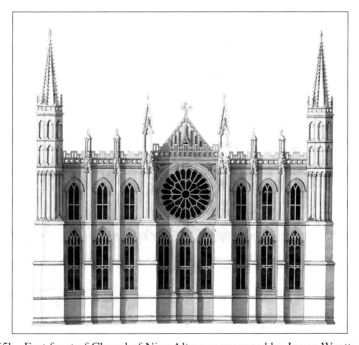

Fig. 55b. East front of Chapel of Nine Altars as proposed by James Wyatt, 1795

Inside the church the 14th century Neville Screen was to be removed to allow the presbytery to be extended into the eastern crossing of the Nine Altars, the new free-standing high altar being screened all round by canopied parclosing. The 17th century organ screen would be swept away to make room for a new screen in the more fashionable Gothic style of the period, and composed of elements derived from, if not physically salvaged from, the Neville Screen and Hatfield Monument. The whole screen was then to be surmounted by an elegant new Gothic organ case, for which the east and west elevations were given.

Externally the western towers were to receive the pinnacles and open parapets originally proposed by Wooler and Nicholson, but the central tower was to receive the most startling of Wyatt's proposed 'improvements'. The belfry stage of the tower was to be crowned by an upper octagonal stage supported by flying buttresses and surmounted by a short spire, very similar to one of Wyatt's designs for the tower at Fonthill Abbey, on which he had stated work in the same year.

Wyatt is said to have pronounced the chapter house ruinous, and in November 1795 the Dean and Chapter ordered it to be taken down, instructing Morpeth to build a 'chapter room' on the site. [12] Wyatt's original plan had shown the chapter house reduced in length but still with an apsidal east end, but this scheme was not followed by Morpeth, the often repeated story being that the latter demolished the chapter house vault by having the keystones knocked out, so allowing it to collapse onto the floor and ancient tomb-slabs below. During 1796 preparations were being made for demolishing the Galilee, but by the end of the year the Chapter had reversed its earlier decision and repaired the roof, largely because of public opinion, due to the activities of John Carter in the Society of Antiquities of London, on whose behalf he had begun to make measured record drawings of the cathedral in 1795.

The folio of drawings includes two designs for the east front of the Nine Altars Chapel. The first belongs to the original set as listed in Wyatt's fee account, and shows the façade almost exactly as reconstructed, with the 15th century tracery eliminated from all the lancet windows, but retaining the 15 century tracery forms of the rose window surrounded by sunk blank cusping. The upper parts of the great central buttresses were to be trimmed down, and the large canopied niches, which Hutchinson's plate had shown containing colossal figures, were to be eliminated.[13] The second drawing presents a much more fanciful design with elaborate pinnacles to the immediate buttresses, and retaining the 15th century tracery in all the windows – much more the sort of design which might have appealed to 18th century clients (Fig.55a,b).

The likely sequence of repair operations on the east front is that Nicholson had started paring down and re-dressing the buttresses, and may have begun to renew the external window dressings, nook-shafts and arches, including the Perpendicular tracery filling the lancets. Certainly the renewed jambs of the lower lancets do have later piecings-in at exactly the points where the tracery and transoms of the 15th century-type windows would occur and which still survive (though renewed) in the south windows of the Nine Altars Chapel. Wyatt probably decided to restore the lancets to their original form, as shown in his first drawing of 1795, and this was the design which Morpeth eventually followed in completing the upper parts of the façade including replacing the old lead-covered spirelet on the south-east turret with the present stone one. The tracery of the rose window was renewed, following the overall design of the 15th century tracery which had replaced the early tracery in the 13th century oculus, but not necessarily following the 15th century details. Wooler's recent north-east spire was left alone. A significant change in the repairs was that Wyatt (or Morpeth) decided to reface the upper parts of the east front in new stone rather than dressing back the old surfaces, so setting the pattern for the re-facings which were to proceed all along the south side of the cathedral during the next fifty years.

James Wyatt's total bill for his work for the Dean and Chapter came to £210 10s. 0d., made up of £150 for his survey in 1795, £100 for providing the set of designs in 1795 and £10.10s. in 1797 for supplying detailed drawings for the work on the east front. As with the Wooler and Nicholson repairs, it is quite evident that Wyatt acted as the outside consultant or adviser, and that the executant architect was Morpeth.

There are several references to slating in the Chapter Minutes 1798-1803, but these simple entries conceal completely the extent of Morpeth's work on the main roofs. He removed entirely the ancient oak high-pitched nave roof, shown in Carter's long section, and replaced it with the present lower pitched queen-post roof, with the ridge line brought down to match those of the quire and transepts. The old nave roof-line can still be distinguished on the west face of the central tower, and in the steep west gable of the nave between the western towers, where the gable apex now stands some ten feet above the new ridge. Morpeth's treatment of the quire roof was not quite so drastic – here he left the old late-medieval collared and strutted trusses and their purlins in position. The lead coverings of the nave, quire and Nine Altars roofs were replaced with Lakeland slates at this time, the change of material seemingly having been suggested by Wyatt. The sale of the lead at this date would have virtually paid for the new slating.

The other work in progress on the cathedral at this time was the construction of the open parapets and 'ragged pinnacles' (ie crocketted pinnacles) on the western towers, originally suggested by Wooler and revived in Wyatt's proposals. An engraving published in 1801 indicates that the parapets were already in position on the north-west tower.[14] The old late medieval revestry on the south side of the quire was also demolished in 1801-02 under Morpeth's direction, in what was to be a long continuing and ill-advised campaign to denude the cathedral of its surviving later medieval additions and insertions, all intended to restore the building to its original and pure 'Norman' state.

In 1803 attention was being turned towards the condition of the great tower, and in 1804 the Chapter sought the advice of another consultant, William Atkinson (1773-1839). Born in Bishop Auckland, he attracted the attention of Wyatt and must have trained under him as well as at the Royal Academy Schools. His report to the Dean and Chapter dated 1804 is of the greatest interest in that it illustrates the changing attitudes to 'Restoration' and the reaction against the masonry re-dressing of Wooler and Nicholson. [18] He was anxious to retain the mossy and ancient appearance of the tower, q1uoting from Burke on the 'Sublime', and to help achieve this, he proposed the use of Parker's Cement. Inside the cathedral he condemned the then current regular re-limewashing of the stonework, and made proposals for increasing the number of seats in the quire, which was a pressing need.

On Atkinson's recommendation, the well-known Italian plaster Francesco Bernasconi was engaged, and work stated on the south side of the tower in 1806, the Chapter stipulating that Atkinson and Bernasconi "include in their estimate the charge of producing the Effect of Roughness and the Appearance of Antiquity." [15]   the work on plastering or cementing the tower proceeded through 1807, but by the summer of 1808 some members of the Chapter were dissatisfied with the results being achieved, and the work was suspended. On 20th July 1809 it was agreed to settle Mr Atkinson's and Mr Bernasconi's bills, and this brought to an end Atkinson's well-intentioned but less than fortunate connection with the cathedral. All the cement work had to be removed from the upper stages of the tower under the direction of Scott in the 1850s, but some of the Parker's Cement statues with brick cores still survive in the refectory undercroft, and the cement is indeed harder than many natural stones. (The fronts of the two prebendal houses, Nos. 9 and 12 The College, were refaced at this time using the Cement, and illustrate the qualities and limitations of the material.)

Purifications, 1827 to 1858

The next main phase of restoration work was to start in 1827 with John Banks Jenkinson, Bishop of St David's, as dean 1827-40, and was to entail the resurfacing of practically the whole south front of the cathedral in new stone, in contrast to the dressing back of the north front masonry under previous regimes. The work was commenced on the south front and gable of the Nine Altars and the south-west buttress of the chapel, picking up at the point where Morpeth had rebuilt the upper part of the south-east turret in 1812-13. Thomas Jackson was the mason contractor for the work, and Ignatius Bonomi was to be the supervising or consultant architect. Bonomi (1787-1870) was a Durham-based architect who had an extensive practice in Durham, Northumberland and Yorkshire in the first half of the 19th century, confident in a number of styles to suit the occasion. It was not surprising, therefore, that he made a careful restoration of the 15th century tracery to the four pairs of lancets in the south wall of the Nine Altars Chapel. For the reconstruction of the gable itself he used the grouped lancets of the 13th century St Edmund's Chapel, Gateshead. His design for rebuilding the south-west turret and spire of the Chapel is more elaborate than the south-east turret by Wyatt or Morpeth, and he made a very positive effort to reproduce the original mouldings and caps, and the bird and beast enrichments, which are one of the delights of closely examining the surviving high-level sculpture of the Nine Altars interior.

Bonomi's restoration at the south end of the Nine Altars was carried out in new natural sandstone, as Wyatt's upper east end had been, this method being followed in all the further restoration work on the cathedral during the remainder of the 19th century. The stone used by Bonomi has weathered to a golden brown colour, and he used similar stone in his restorations of the south clerestory of the quire, and in the south gable and west face of the south transept 1830-35. He also provided the design for reconstructing the east wall of the slype, and took the first steps in opening up the interlacing arcading in the chapter house, which had been hidden behind the lath and plaster of Morpeth's 'Chapter Room'.

Anthony Salvin (1799-1881) succeeded Bonomi as consultant architect, and though of a Durham family in origin, he had been a pupil of John Nash, and his extensive practice remained

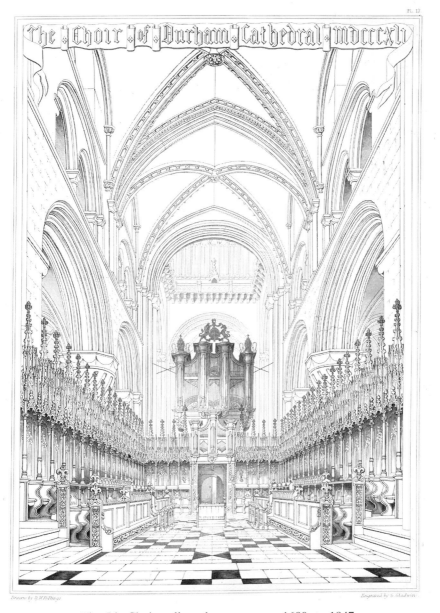

Pl. 13

Fig. 56. Choir stalls and organ screen, 1680s to 1847

London-based. Much of his work for the cathedral – and recently created university - was delegated to the Chapter's Clerk of Works. Salvin was engaged initially to design the new Grammar School, and contracts for building the school were let in May 1843. In the same month he was urgently consulted about the failure of part of the crypt vault beneath the prebendal house which at that time was situated in the southern part of the dormitory. His scheme for the essential repairs was put in hand speedily.

George Jackson, as Clerk of Works, had begun the restoration of the Decorated windows of the quire south aisle in March 1842, the work being carried out in a hard sandstone from Gateshead Fell. Jackson died in September of the same year, and was succeeded by George Pickering, who carried on the work of restoring the eastern aisle of the south transept. Here, for the first time, the later medieval traceried windows were removed and "replaced by the original Norman windows, traces of which were discovered." [16]

In the meantime, under the influence of George Waddington as dean (1840-69), many changes were being made inside the cathedral as fundamental and in many ways as disastrous for the interior of the cathedral, as those of the Reformation and the civil war.` The regular worship was still constricted within the quire by the great organ screen and the return stalls (Fig.56). Several attempts had been made to increase the number of sittings for the congregation in the choir stalls, and in 1844 Pickering prepared a further scheme which added 22 more stalls and 30 sittings. [17]

In 1844 the Tudor screen round the feretory "of indifferent workmanship" [18] was removed (renewed in the 1930s), while in 1845 the marble font and its canopy were removed to the south-west corner of the nave so that the blocked west doorway could be opened up, to be filled by the present oak door, of Pickering's design. What had survived of the 15th century oak screen-work round the Langley tomb was also taken down. The Castel clock case, "of carved oak of inferior workmanship", [19] was removed from the south transept (also restored in the 1930s). Salvin designed a new stone pulpit for the quire in 1845, and new stone and marble altar rails in 1849. Mr Raine, the Chapter Librarian, had provided the design for a 'Norman' font in 1846, which was executed in Caen stone by Mr White of Pimlico. White also re-sorted the Neville Screen, and in 1849 was commissioned to execute in Caen stone an altarpiece of 'Leonardo da Vinci's Last Supper' to be erected above the high altar. [20]
(This reredos is now stored in the triforium.)

1847 was momentous for the interior of the cathedral, for the organ screen - "a work of Charles ll's time, in oak and not unskilfully carved, but after designs wholly inappropriate to a place of worship" [21] - was removed and the organ resited on the north side of the choir (Fig. 57). Such actions illustrate the mid-19th century attitude to how a great cathedral interior should be treated, banishing monuments and fittings which were not in the taste of the period. Salvin has been blamed for much that was done, but though his advice may have been sought unofficially, the quire pulpit and altar rails are the only items specifically linked with his name in the Chapter Minutes at this time.

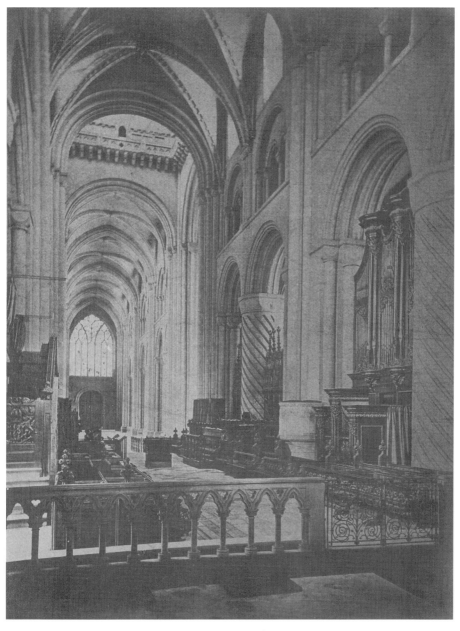

Fig. 57. Choir 1847-70, minus organ screen and with 17th century organ cut down and placed on
    north side

During these years of internal re-arrangements to furnishings in the cathedral, work had been proceeding steadily on the fabric itself. In 1847 Salvin was renewing the window tracery of the large Decorated windows to the north quire aisle. Rather than restore the windows in their existing forms, which he must have considered debased, Salvin introduced three designs of his own, derived from windows in Sleaford and Holbeach in Linolnshire and Boushton Aluph in Kent. Stained glass had been provided for the rose window in 1839, and for the north window of the Nine Altars in 1847. The same year saw removal of the tracery from the windows to the north clerestory of the quire, and they were restored to their original Norman forms, as were all the windows of the north triforium of the nave. Work continued with the windows of the north side of the Nave in 1848, the Perpendicular tracery being removed and the original Norman surrounds and nook-shafts restored, and plain glass inserted. The windows at the western extremities of the north and south aisles were also deprived of their tracery and restored to their Norman forms. [22]

George Pickering reported to Chapter in 1849 on the serious state of the external masonry to the south aisle of the nave. The total re-facing of the aisle in new stone followed, under his direction, the proposals being subject to the approval by Salvin. All the later Gothic traceried windows were changed back to Norman, and the evidence of earlier gablets to the aisle was obliterated, though Salvin did produce a scheme for restoring the aisle gables. The nave north and south clerestories were also refaced, and their windows lost their tracery, all this Pickering work being done in a grey stone. In due course this cycle of window 'restoration' was completed with the east aisle of the north transept, only the west face of this transept escaping, thereby preserving something of the charm of later medieval tracery within Romanesque window surrounds. The cathedral is indeed fortunate that much of the original medieval window tracery has survived in the 'terminal' windows, at the west end and in the transepts. There never seems to have been any intention of restoring the conjectural Romanesque windows to the end gables of the nave and transepts.

Scholarly Repairs, 1858 to 1933

The next major work on the cathedral was to be the restoration of the belfry stage of the central tower, for ever since Atkinson's cement-work repairs to the belfry had been summarily suspended by the Chapter in 1808, the appearance of the tower must have been of concern. The Great Chapter of 20th November 1858 therefore agreed that the upper parapet be restored in stone "according to plans to be approved by Mr Gilbert Scott of London…..the celebrated medieval Architect." [29] (The future Sir George Gilbert Scott (1811-78) was the most successful Gothic Revival architect of his generation; by the end of his career he had carried out restoration or furnishing work on at least twenty English and Welsh cathedrals.) Scott was also asked to submit plans and specifications for the eventual restoration of the belfry and removal of the cement. His proposals were accepted in 1859, and the work completed the next year, with the entire belfry being refaced in Prudham and Dunhouse stone.

A special Chapter was held on 6th March 1860 to consider Gilbert Scott's designs for the termination of the central tower. [24] Just as his predecessors, Wooler, Nicholson and Wyatt had felt the need to 'improve' the top of the central tower, so did Scott. His proposals were even

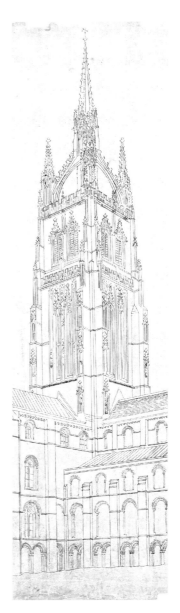

Fig. 58a. Central tower proposals
James Wyatt, 1795

Fig. 58b. Central tower proposals, Sir George
Gilbert Scott, 1860

more startling than those of Wyatt (Figs.58 a,b). His intention was to construct an open crown on flying buttresses supported by great pinnacles, similar to but on a larger scale than the 15th corona of St Nicholas, Newcastle, which Scott was to restore so expertly. However, the Chapter restricted Scott to heightening the pierced battlements and the little square pinnacles surmounting the corner buttresses. This preserved the unique tapering silhouette of the Durham tower which is given by the canopied offsets of its slender corner buttresses. It was the Chapter's Clerk of Works and deputy to Scott, who advised the Chapter to reject Scott's scheme, mainly on structural grounds, and in this he was almost certainly right.

Edward Robert Robson (1836-1917), a Durham man and son of a local builder who had trained with Dobson in Newcastle and Scott in London, proceeded with repairs to the west face and north-west corner of the Galilee Chapel in 1863, and may have been responsible for the careful restoration of the north door to the chapel. He was succeeded as Clerk of Works by Charles Hodgson Fowler, another of Scott's proteges. Hodgson Fowler continued the work on the Galilee Chapel and prepared schemes for various work on College houses. He reported on fractures in a pinnacle and several pilasters of the western towers in 1866, but the Chapter made no immediate decision on them. However, restoration of the exterior of the College gate was commenced in 1867. In the same year the great western window and south transept window were filled with stained glass, retaining the surviving medieval painted glass in some of the tracery lights.

In 1870 Sir Gilbert Scott was recalled to Durham. Within six years the triple-arched marble quire screen was built and the Cosmati work marble pulpit provided, together with the letten brass Pelican lectern. [25]   But the most important contributions at this time were Scott's superb marble pavement to the quire and sanctuary in Opus Alxandrium, and the restoration of the choir stalls and tabernacle canopies to something very like their 17th century arrangements, after having been cut up and set back in the 1840s. Scott was now towards the end of his career, and at least where the stalls are concerned, some of the credit for their restoration must be attributable to his pupil, Hodgson Fowler, who would have been in charge of the work.

Much criticism has been levelled at Scott's quire screen during those years when High Victorian design was out of favour. Yet in the thirty years between the removal of the organ screen and the erection of the new screen, the 'grand vista' from west to east in the cathedral had come to be considered somewhat disappointing and lacking in visual punctuation. The Scott screen is simple and bold in concept, and whatever one thinks of its detailed design, it does provide the necessary element that had been missing and which gives incident and scale to the whole interior of the building.

During the middle years of the 19th century a series of ecclesiastical reforms were affecting all cathedral chapters, and one of the results was that the Architect to the Ecclesiastical Commissioners, Ewan Christian, visited Durham in 1870 to assess the state of the cathedral fabric and cost of repairs required within the next twenty years. Christian's report of 1st December 1870 deplored the "Wyatt" repairs (Everyone continued to blame Wyatt for the Wooler and Nicholson re-dressing until the 1950s), and rightly pointed out that the cutting away of the stone surfaces would lead to much more difficult repair problems in the future. He was concerned about the state of the internal flying buttresses to the triforia, but gave first priority to repairs needed to the open arcading in the upper parts of the western towers. These he considered would cost £14,000, and should be undertaken immediately. He commented on the poor stat of some of the lead-covered roofs, and inside the cathedral he commented, as Atkinson had done in 1804, on the need to remove the encrustations of white-wash from the stonework, and noted this had been done successfully at that time in the south aisle.

Most of the works on which Christian reported were to be carried out in the following years. The remainder of the internal stonework was cleaned of the whitewash or limewash in all but the least visible parts of the building, and the upper arcading of the western towers was extensively renewed. This work on the towers will have been undertaken by Hodgson Fowler, and it was he who designed the twin organ cases in the quire surmounting the stall canopies.

Hodgson Fowler was made Architect to the Dean and Chapter in 1885, and he is best remembered for his reconstruction of the chapter house as a memorial to Bishop Lightfoot in 1892. Some work had been commissioned on restoring the chapter house in 1847 when the western entrance, sealed up by Morpeth, was re-opened, and some of the arcading, which had been hidden by lath and plaster, was revealed. In 1857 the great west window to the chapter house had been re-opened, and the west wall restored, in association with repair work in the cloister. Hodgson Fowler had a fair amount of evidence on which to base his design for the rebuilding the eastern apse of the chapter house in the form of engravings. But for some reason he did not quite follow the plan of the apse ribs, for his keystone at the junction of the apse ribs differs in certain details from the original keystone, which still survives. Of use in structural terms is his use of concrete for the vault cells rather than rubble masonry – one of his few concessions to more modern constructional methods, even if he did use the material in much the way that Roman engineers would have one.

Mervyn, later Sir Mervyn, Edmund Macartney succeeded Hodgson Fowler, and submitted reports on the state of the cathedral. At the same time William Douglas Caroe, who had succeeded Ewan Christian as Architect to the Ecclesiastical Commissioners, made a detailed structural examination in 1913 in which he expressed particular concern about the condition of the distorted semi-arches over the quire triforia, and the quadrant flying buttresses of the nave triforium.

In 1915 major repairs were begun on the nave vault, following the reports by Macarrtney and Caroe. Under the direction of the former, two extra rings of stone were inserted under the nave triforium quadrant arches, making them into very solid internal flying buttresses to abut the thrust from the nave vault, while steel tie rods were placed above the high vault to restrain any outward movement in the clerestory walls. This work caused an absolute storm within the Society of Antiquities of London, and the Society commissioned three fellows to report.[26] They agreed that the work was unnecessary and was destroying the historical integrity of the structure. We have no record of Macartney's views, but at least the rent in the nave vault originally reported by Wooler was solidly repaired, and no movement has shown itself in the nave structure, and yet virtually nothing has been done to them since 1913, and they seem none the worse for it.

In his 1913 report Caroe had expressed concern about the central tower and the lantern vault, partly because of the design of the structure, and partly from the effects of bell ringing. He amplified his concern in a further report in July 1922, and was commissioned by the Chapter to undertake the necessary structural repairs that year. Displaced vault-rib stones were eased back into place, cracks in the ringing chamber walls were cement-grouted and stitched with tiles, while the whole bell frame and its supporting structure were tightened up and braced as far as possible. The project inside the cathedral for which Caroe was responsible at this time was the design of the Durham Light Infantry memorial Chapel and its elaborate oak screening. The marble monument listing all the bishops, priors and deans of Durham was designed in 1929by wood and Oakley, who were the successors of C.H. Fowler's practice, and they also modified the oak parclose screens either side of the sanctuary. Outside, the parapets and pinnacles of the two western towers were reconstructed 1930-33 under the direction of Reginald Annandale Cordingley, the head of the School of Architecture in Newcastle. It was at this period that there had been considerable concern over the stability of the Galilee Chapel, at a time when extensive engineering works were found necessary to prevent the castle slipping towards the river.

Care and Concern, 1933 to the end of the Millennium

The advent of dean Alington may be taken as the beginning of the modern period, characterised by efforts to rectify what in our conservation-conscious era we deem the ravages of the past. Thus, the remaining fragments of the 17th century screen and organ were assembled near the west end of the south aisle under Cordingsley's direction, while the feretory sreen was renewer, copying sections which had survived.The elegant 17th century marble font was brought out of retirement from Pittinton, and the most important, the Castel Clock was reinstated in the south transept. Dean Alington listened to the advice of Stephen Dykes Bower for much of this work, and it was he who designed the silver cross and candlesticks for the Bede Altar in the Chapel of the Nine Altars in 1935. As successors to Cordingley, Donald McIntyre and Matthew Hayton had designed the oak 'birdcage' lectern in 1939, which supplanted Scott's brass pelican until 1990, and which was intended to have a tall 'Cosin Gothic' canopy.

After 1945, with John Wild as dean, it was Sir Ninian Comper (1864-1960) who was to design the hanging tester over the feretory, with Donald McIntyre (until 1969) and Matthew Hayton (until 1973) continuing as resident architects to the cathedral, and with George Gaze Pace (1915-75) as Consultant Architect from 1955 until his death. Pace was exceedingly active, with a series of repairs and additions very much in the Durham idiom. (At the same time he inserted a large new university library between the cathedral and castle (1966), a daunting challenge which won universal acclaim.) Major repair to the stonework was undertaken to the Priory Kitchen in 1969, while the north-west spirelet of the Nine Altars Chapel was rebuilt in 1962. New underfloor heating was installed 1967-69. He designed the new gold and ebony reredos in the Gregory Chapel in 1959, restored the 17th century choir pulpit in 1964, and designed the Galilee cross and Bede memorial in 1967 and 1970, respectively. His were the designs for reglazing the north aisle of the nave, the Galilee Chapel and refectory 1965-70, the new gateway to the Deanery in 1974 and the display bookcases in the spendement in 1975. The first significant contribution to visitor hospitality came with his last piece in 1976, when the south end of the undercroft was converted from an open windy store to a restaurant and bookshop.

The first contribution of Pace's successor, Ian Curry, was to design a new treasury in the adjoining middle section of the undercroft (1978), followed by reconstruction of the choir music library on the site of the revestry (1985) and positioning new oak lobbies to the north and south doors in the cathedral. Outside, there was extensive re-slating of the quire and Nine Altars roofs 1972-77, during which the 1830 refaced masonry of the south quire clerestory had to be re-secured to the core walling. There followed re-slating of the nave and north transept roofs 1987-90. The use of Lakeland slate meant that like was replaced with like.

In 1982 a long-term programme of masonry repairs was begun, to include all the stonework that was redressed or cut back at the end of the 18th century. Work continued in a progression from the southern end of the Nine Altars, to the east front and then the north front, eventually to reach the western towers. Inside the cathedral the plasterwork of the quire vaults were repaired, cleaned and redecorated 1990-91. In the central tower the bells were re-hung in a new frame in 1980, the 1922 stiffening of the old framework having proved ineffective. The intermediate pinnacles of the central tower were extensively repaired 1990-91 since the stones used in the 1865 repairs had eroded to an alarming extent. All these repairs were now taking place to a World Heritage Site, the cathedral, along with the castle, having been inscribed on the UNESCO list in 1986. More directly, under the Care of Cathedrals Measure of 1990, a statutory national body was set up – the Cathedrals Fabric Commission for England – with control over certain types of work, along with a Fabric Advisory Committee for the cathedral. In 1992 the first Quinquennial Report on the Cathedral Church and Claustral Buildings was prepared, as required under the Measure.

Apart from continuing masonry repairs, the 1990s brought roof repairs to the dormitory (1993), dismantling and rebuilding of the north-east pinnacle and spirelet of the Nine Altars (1995-6), rebuilding chimney stacks on the chapter house and prior's hall (1996) and, not least, transfer of the bookshop to a new home in the Great Kitchen and Covey (allowing the restaurant to double in size). The bookshop was opened in December 1997, within months of Christopher Downs succeeding Ian Curry his former senior partner, as Architect

The first years of the new millennium were noted for repairing the roof of roof the Refectory (2007) and of the south side of Prior's Hall, along with stone repairs (2009). In 2010 the east end of the south quire brought saw the insertion of a large stained glass window of the Transfiguration by Tom Denny as a memorial to Archbishop Michael Ramsey. In 2011the Deanery Undercroft was restored as a Chapel of the Holy Spirit. Christopher Downs resigned in the same year. New flood-lighting of the exterior of cathedral was installed in 2012. For forty years the building had been washed with a general light; in the replacement scheme the architectural detail is etched and highlighted to great effect by its more selective illumination.

The Present

It is more than evident that a mere forty years of Anglo-Norman building set in motion centuries of Romanesque aftercare, which will continue to provide a never-ending challenge.

The present generation, however, will also benefit from the results of a long-term development plan which has set in train the most far-reaching series of changes since the Victorian era.

Christopher Cotton was appointed Project Architect - later Cathedral Architect - in 2012. He and his colleagues from Purcell, Architects of York, produced two detailed surveys, one of the cathedral and another for the claustral buildings,[27] for a project which the cathedral chapter termed 'Open Treasure'. The aim of the management plan is to offer all categories of visitor a more coherent welcome and hospitality, an integral part of which is a legible 'route map' through the buildings to open up its inherited treasures through exhibition and interpretation. To this end, the dormitory undercroft has already seen the re-sitng of the choir vestry and treasury, so that the whole length of the crypt vaults has been opened up (2012). At the southern end there remains the restaurant, divided only by a glass lobby from a new bookshop at the northern end. A new exhibition space will be provided in the monks' dormitory, while the most priceless treasures, incorporating Cuthbert's relics, will be in the Great Kitchen. Inner glazed doors are proposed for both the north and south doors of the cathedral, the latter to facilitate finding the monastic buildings, where new passage-ways, a lift, together with signage, will enable the visitor to appreciate fully the genius that is Durham.

REFERENCES

Chapter 1

[1] Anon., 'The world's best buildings,' part 1, *The Illustrated London News* (May 1984), 50-57.

[2] D.W.Rollason, Cuthbert, *Saint and Patron*, Dean & Chapter, Durham (1987)

[3] Jean Bony, The stonework planning of the first Durham Master', in Eric Fernie and Paul Crossley (eds), *Medieval Architecture and its Intellectual Context: Studies in Honour of Peter Kidson*, The Hambledon Press, London, (1990), 19-34.

[4] Sherban Cantacuzino, 'An architectural appreciation,' in Douglas Pocock (ed) *Durham Cathedral: A Celebration*, City of Durham Trust, Durham (1993), 68-73.

[5] Thomas E. Russo, 'The Romanesque rood screen of Durham Cathedral: context and form', in D.W. Rollason Margaret Harvey, Michael Prestwich (eds), *Anglo-Norman Durham* Boydell Press, Woodbridge (1993), 251-68.

[6] K.J.Conant, *Carolingian and Romanesque Architecture 800-1200* (Penguin History of Art), London, 2nd edition (1990), 459.

[7] C.R.Peers, J. Bilson, H. Brakspear, 'A Report to the Societies of Antiquities on certain repairs now being undertaken at Durham Cathedral', *Proceedings of the Society of Antiquities 2nd series*, XXVIII (1915-16), 49-53, and letters following.

[8] N. Pevsner, *Outline of European Architecture*, Penguin: Harmondsworth (1963), 66.

[9] N. Pevsner (revised by E. Williamson), *The Buildings Of England: County Durham*, Penguin: Harmondsworth (1983), 159-60.

[10] Stephen Games, Pevsner: *The Early Life: Germany and Art*, London: Continuum International Publishing: London (2010), 159.

[11] H.V. Morton, *In Search of England*, Methuen: London (1927), 205.

[12] Simon Jenkins, *The Sunday Times*, 3rd April, 2005.

[13] Alec Clifton-Taylor, *Another Six English Towns*, BBC: London (1984), 181.

[14] R.W. Chapman (ed), *The Letters of Samuel Johnson*, Clarendon Press: Oxford (1952), Vol.1, 339.

[15] Sir Roy Strong, *The Illustrated London News*, op.cit., 51.

[16] Bill Bryson, *Notes from a Small Island*, Black Swan: London (1996), 295.

[17] *Northern Echo*, 15th July 1944.

[18] T.G. Jackson, *Byzantine and Romanesque Architecture*, Cambridge University Press: Cambridge (1913), vol 2, 223.

[19] F.H. Rushford, *City Beautiful: A Vision of Durham*, County Advertiser: Durham (1944).

[20] N. Pevner (revised by E. Williamson), *op. cit.*, 160.   .

[21] Douglas Pocock, *In the Steps of the Masters: Durham in Paintings*, City of Durham Trust: Durham (2010); Douglas Pocock, 'The Cathedral in Art,' in David Brown (ed), *Durham Cathedral: History, Fabric and Culture*, Yale University Press: London, (2014).

[22] Simon Jenkins, *England's 100 Best Views*, Profile Books: London (2013), 298.

[23] Alec Clifton-Taylor, *ibid.*, 205.

[24] Thomas Sharp, *Cathedral City: A Plan for Durham City,* Architectural Press, London (1945), 88-9.

Chapter 2

[1]   On Speyer Cathedral, see Hans Erich Kubach and Walter Haas, *Der Dom zu Speyer*, 3 vols, Munich (1972); Dethard von Winterfeld, *Palatinat roman*, La Pierre-qui-Vire [Yonne] (1993), 63-120; Peter Kidson, "The Mariakirk at Utrecht, Speyer and Italy", *Utrecht, Britain and the Continent, Archaeology, Art and Architecture: The British Archaeological Association Conference Transactions*, XVIII, ed. Elisabeth de Bièvre, Leeds (1996), 123-136. Dethard von Winterfeld, "The Imperial Cathedrals of Speyer, *Mainz and Worms: The Current State of Research*", *Mainz and the Middle Rhine Valley, Medieval Art, Architecture and Archaeology: The British Archaeological Association Conference Transactions*, XXX, ed. Ute Engel and Alexandra Gajewski, Leeds (2007), 14-32; on *Cluny, Kenneth John Conant, Cluny, les églises et la maison du chef d'ordre*, Macon (1968); on Romanesque St Albans abbey, Malcolm Thurlby, *"L'abbatiale romane de St. Albans", in L'architecture normande au Moyen Age*, 2 vols. ed. Maylis Baylé, Caen (1997), I, 79-90; Eric Fernie, *The Architecture of Norman England*, Oxford (2000), 111-15.

[2]   This opinion was challenged by David McGee, "The 'early vaults' of Saint-Etienne at Beauvais", *Journal of the Society of Architectural Historians*, XLV (1986), 20-31.

[3]   For a review of the literature on this point, and a convincing alternative interpretation of the quadrant arches, see Stephen Gardner, "The nave galleries of Durham Cathedral," *Art Bulletin*, LXIV (1982), 564-79.

[4]   For convenient summaries, see M.G. Snape, "Documentary evidence for the building of Durham Cathedral and its monastic buildings" *Medieval Art and Architecture at Durham Cathedral: British Archaeological Association Conference Transactions*, III, ed. Nicola Coldstream and Peter Draper, Leeds (1980), 20-36; David Rollason, "Durham Cathedral 1093-1193 sources and history", in *Engineering a Cathedral*, ed. Michael J. Jackson, London (1993), 1-15.

[5]   K.W. Markuson, "Recent investigation in the east range of the cathedral monastery, Durham", Medieval Art and Architecture (1980), op. cit. note 4, 37-48.

[6]   W.H. St John Hope, "Notes on recent excavations in the cloister of Durham abbey," *Proceedings of the Society of Antiquaries of London*, 2nd ser., XXII (1909), 416-23.

[7]   David Rollason, ed. & trans., *Symeon of Durham, Libellus de exordio atque procursu istius, hoc est dunhelmensis, ecclesie*, Oxford (2000), 244/245.

[8]   John Bilson, "The east end of Durham Cathedral", *Journal of the Royal Institute of British Architects*, II, (1896), 546-48; John Bilson, "Recent discoveries at the east end of Durham Cathedral", *Archaeological Journal*, LII (1896), 1-18.

[9]   Eric Fernie, "The effect of the Conquest on Norman architectural patronage", *Anglo-Norman Studies*, IX (1986), 71-85.

[10]   Eric Fernie, "The Spiral Piers of Durham Cathedral", *Medieval Art and Architecture* (1980), op. cit. note 4, 49-58; Malcolm Thurlby, 'The Roles of the Patron and the Master Mason in the First Design of Durham Cathedral', in *Anglo-Norman Durham* 1093-1193, ed. David Rollason et al, Woodbridge (1994), 161-184.

[11]   Friedrich Wilhelm Deichmann, 'Säule und Ordnung in der frühchristlichen Architektur', *Römische Mitteilungen*, 55 (1940), 114-130, reprinted in Friedrich Wilhelm Deichmann,

Rom, Ravenna, Konstantinopel, Naher Osten: Gesammelte studien zur spätantiken Architektur, Kunst und Geschichte, Wiesbaden (1982), 159-186; Beat Brenk, 'Spolia from Constantine to Charlemagne: Aesthetics versus Ideology', *Dumbarton Oaks Papers*, (1987), 103-109.

[12] John Higgitt, 'The Roman Background to Medieval England', *Journal of the British Archaeological Association*, XXXVI (1973), 1-15 at 10.

[13] British Library, Add.38818 fols.49-109; L.D.Reynolds and S.F. Weiskittel, "Vitruvius", in *Texts and Transmission: A Survey of the Latin Classics*, ed. L.D. Reynolds, Oxford (1983) 440-45 at 443; Carol Herselle Krinsky, "Seventy-Eight Vitruvius Manuscripts", Journal of the Warburg and Courtauld Institutes, 30 (1967), 36- 70 at 49; John Hooper Harvey, The Mediæval Architect, London (1972), 21.

[14] John Bilson, "Durham Cathedral: the chronology of its vaults", *Archaeological Journal*, LXXIX (1922), 101-60 at 108, suggested that the first master mason at Durham may have "been employed on one of the greater churches in England – such, for example, as Winchester…"

[15] For further discussion, see Malcolm Thurlby, "The Purpose of the Rib in the Romanesque Vaults of Durham Cathedral", in *Engineering a Cathedral*, ed. Michael J. Jackson, London (1993), 43-63.

[16] Paul Frankl, *The Gothic: Literary Sources and Interpretations through Eight Centuries*, Princeton (1960), 763-72, 798-826.

[17] Robert Mark, *Experiments in Gothic Structure*, Cambridge, Mass (1982), 102-117.

[18] For further discussion of this matter, see Malcolm Thurlby, "Observations on Romanesque and Early Gothic Vault Construction", *Arris*, 6 (1995), 22-29; Lawrence Hoey and Malcolm Thurlby, "A Survey of Romanesque Vaulting in Great Britain and Ireland", *Antiquaries Journal*, 84 (2004), 117-184.

[19] John James, "The rib vaults of Durham Cathedral", *Gesta*, XXII (1983), at 139-40. See also, Thurlby (1995), *op. cit.* note 18.

[20] Bilson (1922), *op. cit.* note 14, 156.

[21] Jean Bony, "Durham et la tradition saxonne', *Études d'art médiévale offertes à Louis Grodecki*, ed. Sumner McK. Crosby, Paris (1981), 79-85; Thurlby, "The Roles of the Patron and the Master Mason," op. cit. note 10; Lisa Reilly, 'The Emergence of Anglo-Norman Architecture: Durham Cathedral', *Anglo-Norman Studies*, XIX (1996), 335-351.

[22] Illustrated in David M. Wilson, *Anglo-Saxon Art from the Seventh Century to the Norman Conquest*, London (1984), ill. 103.

[23] The latter may date from shortly after the Conquest but the constructional details at Hadstock belong to an Anglo-Saxon tradition. See Eric Fernie, 'The Responds and Dating of St Botolph's, Hadstock', *Journal of the British Archaeological Association*, 136 (1983), 62-73.

[24] Fernie, "The Spiral Piers of Durham Cathedral," *op. cit.*, note 10.

[25] John Bilson (1922), op. cit., note 14, 107-108, compared the alternation of major piers and minor columns in the main arcade plus the proportions of the three-storey elevation and the projecting band with a quirked chamfer on its upper and lower edges which runs above the plinth under the external dado arcades of the choir aisles, and on the plinths of the main arcade piers, with the nave of Jumièges Abbey.

[26] Bilson (1922), *op. cit.*, note 14, 123-128.

[27] Gary Schwartz and Marten Jan Bok, Pieter Saenredam, *The Painter and His Time*, New York (1989); Liesbeth M. Helmus, ed., *Pieter Saenredam, The Utrecht Work*, Los Angeles (2002); and Kidson (1996), *op. cit.*, note 1.

[28] John James (1983), suggested a sexpartite vault over double bays but this has not been generally accepted: see Malcolm Thurlby, "The Romanesque high vaults of Durham Cathedral", in *Engineering a Cathedral*, ed. Michael J. Jackson, London (1993), 43-63 at 45-46; Eric Fernie, "Design principles of early medieval architecture as exemplified at Durham Cathedral," in *Engineering a Cathedral*, ed. Michael J. Jackson, London (1993), 146-56 at 153; Paul Frankl, *Gothic Architecture*, 2nd edn., revised by Paul Crossley, New Haven and London (2000), 305 n1, 306 n2., 307 n23.

[29] Bilson (1922), *op. cit.*, note 14, 123-128.

[30] Ian Curry, "Aspects of the Anglo-Norman Design of Durham Cathedral", *Archaeologia Aeliana*, 5th series, XIV (1986), 31-48 at 34, fig. 2.

[31] The latter scheme is reconstructed by John James, *op cit.*, note 19, 144-45, note 11, figs 10 and 11.

[32] Curry (1986), *op. cit.*, note 30, 45, fig. 8.

[33] Thurlby (1993), *op. cit.*, note 10, 169-72, plates 19 and 20. For a reconstruction drawing of the eastern towers, see Michael J. Jarrett and Howard Mason, "'Greater and More Splendid': Some Aspects of Romanesque Durham Cathedral", *Antiquaries Journal*, 75 (1995), 189-233, fig. 6.

[34] Sir Charles Peers, "Peterborough Minster," in *The Victoria History of the Counties of England: Northamptonshire*, II, ed. W.D. Atkins *et al.* (London 1906), 440.

[35] Thurlby (1993), *op. cit.*, note 10, pl. 21.

[36] *Ibid*, pl. 23.

[37] In 1072 Earl Waltheof commenced the castle "where the bishop could enclose himself with his men out of danger from invaders." Bishop Flambard built a curtain wall from the east end of the cathedral up to the castle and leveled the space between them – William Page (ed), *The Victoria History of the Counties of England: Durham*, III, London (1928), 64-93.

[38] The geometry of the Romanesque design is examined in detail by Hugh George McCague, "Durham Cathedral and Medieval Architecture: Manifestation of the Sacred through Number and Geometry", unpublished MA thesis, York University, Toronto (1992).

[39] Illustrated in Thurlby (1993), *op. cit.*, note 15, fig 13. The same principle is found in the north transept of the Romanesque abbey church at Knechsteden (North Rhein – Westphalia) where the pilaster between the two bays of the north wall rises directly to the underside of the high groin vault.

[40] Jean Bony, "Le projet premier de Durham: voûtement partiel ou voûtement total?", in *Urbanisme et architecture: etudes écrites et publiées en honneur de Pierre Lavedan*, Paris (1954), 41-49, argues that transept high vaults were not part of the initial plan. This is followed by Elizabeth Williamson in the revised edition of Nikolaus Pevsner, *The Buildings of England: County Durham*, Harmondsworth (1983), 184-5; Roger Stalley, *Early Medieval Architecture*, Oxford (1999), 140; Fernie (2000), op. cit. note 1, 135-6; Eric Fernie, 'La seconda cattedrale di Durham', Medioevo: *l'Europa della cattedrali: Atti del Convegno internatzionale di studi Parma, 19-23 settembre 2006* (Milan: Electa 2007), 132-140. Contrary to the case presented by both Bony and Fernie, John Bilson, op. cit., note 16, 128-

29, 133-34; William Page, *VCH Durham*, III; and the present author [Thurlby (1993), *op. cit.* note 15, 64-76], suggest that the 1093 design of the church included high vaults in the transepts, an idea accepted by Paul Crossley, *op. cit.* note 28, 307 n. 23A.

41   It has been suggested that vault shafts like those above the main arcade columns in the east elevation could have been included on the west wall by making it thicker from the ground up [Fernie (2000), *op. cit.* note 1, 136]. Of course, that is quite correct but I do not know of a single Romanesque analogue for such thickening of a transept wall simply to facilitate correspondence with articulation on an opposite wall. On the other hand, asymmetry between east and west elevations was commonplace.

42   Bilson (1922) *op. cit.* note 15.

43   On the Anglo-Saxon cathedral, see Eric Cambridge in H.D. Braggs, E. Cambridge and R.N. Bailey, "A new approach to church archaeology: dowsing, excavation and documentary work at Woodhorn, Ponteland and the pre-Norman cathedral at Durham", *Archaeologia Aeliana*, Series 5, 11 (1983), 91-97; and Eric Cambridge, "Early Romanesque architecture in north-east England: a style and its patrons", in *Anglo-Norman Durham 1093-1193*, ed. David Rollason *et al*, Woodbridge (1994), 141-60 at 144-48. The south transept of the Romanesque church of Peterborough abbey (cathedral) was built in part over the eastern arm and transept of the Anglo-Saxon church (H.M. and Joan Taylor, *Anglo-Saxon Architecture*, 2 vols (Cambridge 1965), II, fig. 241.

44   Fernie (2007), *op. cit.* note 40. Meredith Bacola has investigated this matter in detail and I am most grateful to her for sharing a draft of a paper she has prepared for publication.

45   Robert W. Billings, *Architectural Illustrations and Description of the Cathedral Church of Durham*, London (1843), 5.

46   Billings is followed by Charles Herbert Moore, *Development and Character of Gothic Architecture* London and New York (1890), 14 and 17, but he expresses reservations in *The Medieval Church Architecture of England*, New York (1912), 35-3; Francis Bond, *Gothic Architecture in England*, London (1905), 30, 370; E. Lefèvre-Pontalis, "L'origine des arc-boutants," *Congrès archéolgique*, LXXXII (1919), 367-96 at 372-74; Ernst Gall, *Die Gotische Baukunst in Frankreich und Deutschland*, I, (Leipzig 1925), 84; John Bilson (1922), op. cit., note 14, 143-45; Marcel Aubert, "Les plus anciennes croisées d'ogives. Leur role dans la construction, *Bulletin Monumental*, XCIII (1934), 6-67 and 137-237 at 27; Henri Focillon, *Art of the West in the Middle Ages, II, Gothic*, London (1963), 12; James Acland, *Medieval Structure: The Gothic Vault*, Toronto (1972), 92. Against Billings, see Kenneth John Conant, *Carolingian and Romanesque Architecture*, Harmondsworth (1966), 290; Louis Grodecki, *Gothic Architecture*, New York (1977), 39.

47   Crossley in revised edition of Frankl, *op. cit.* note 28, 305 n1. It should be noted that the two inner orders of the quadrant arches were added in 1915; see C.H. Peers, John Bilson and Harold Brakspear, "A Report to the Society of Antiquaries on certain repairs now being undertaken at Durham Cathedral", *Proceedings of the Society of Antiquaries of London*, 2nd ser., XXVIII (1915-16), 49-53, plus ensuing letters and comments, 53-56.

48   Lindy Grant, *Architecture and Society in Normandy*, New Haven and London (2005), 46, 56.

49   Stephen Gardner, 'The Nave Galleries of Durham Cathedral', *Art Bulletin*, 64 (1982), 564-79. Eric Fernie, 'The Architectural Influence of Durham Cathedral', in *Anglo-Norman Durham 1093-1193*, ed. David Rollason *et al*, Woodbridge (1994), 269-79 at 277-8 suggests

that the quadrant arches could not have acted as buttresses.

50 J. Philip McAleer, "The north portal of Durham Cathedral and the problem of 'sanctuary' in Medieval Britain", *Antiquaries Journal*, 81 (2001), 195-258.

51 J. Philip McAleer, "Romanesque England and the development of the *façade harmonique*," Gesta, XXIII/2 (1984), 87-105.

52 Peter Fergusson and Stuart Harrison, *Rievaulx Abbey*, New Haven and London (1999),

53 For colour illustrations of the Franks Casket, see Wilson (1984, *op. cit.* note 22, ills 34-37.

54 On links between England, Normandy and Spain after the capture of Toledo in 1085, see Jean Bony, 'The Stonework Planning of the First Durham Master', *Medieval Architecture in its Intellectual Context: Studies in Honour of Peter Kidson*, ed. Eric Fernie and Paul Crossley, London and Ronceverte (1990), 19-34 at 33-34.

55 Richard Gem and Malcolm Thurlby, "The Early Monastic Church of Lastingham", in *Yorkshire Monasticism: Archaeology, Art and Architecture: British Archaeological Association Conference Transactions*, XVI, ed. Lawrence R. Hoey, Leeds (1995), 31-39.
    Stuart Harrison and Christopher Norton, 'Lastingham and the Architecture of the Benedictine revival in Northumbria', *Anglo-Norman Studies*, 34 (2012), 63-88 at 84-85 argue that the presbytery vault at Lastingham was invented by John Loughborough Pearson in his restoration' of 1877-1879. But the Faculty specifically mentions the restoration of the ancient groining.

56 Curry (1986), *op. cit.* note 30, 34.

57 R.N. Bailey and R.J. Cramp, *Corpus of Anglo-Saxon Stone Sculpture, vol. 2, Cumberland, Westmorland and Lancashire north-of-the-Sands*, Oxford (1988), 106-`08, ills 325, 326 & 328.

58 Malcolm Thurlby, 'Romanesque Architecture and Sculpture in the Diocese of Carlisle', *Carlisle and Cumbria: Roman and Medieval Architecture, Art and Archaeology: British Archaeological Association Conference Transactions*, XXVII, ed. Mike McCarthy, Leeds (2004), 269-290, fig. 10.

59 R.A. Cordingley, 'Norman Decoration in Durham Cathedral', *Archaeologia Aeliana*, 4th series, X (1933), 133-39; Bony, op. cit., note 54, 19-34.

60 Richard Halsey, "The Galilee Chapel", in *Medieval Art and Architecture* (1980), 20-36; Stuart Harrison, 'Observations on the Architecture of the Galilee Chapel', in *Anglo-Norman Durham 1093-1193*, ed. David Rollason *et al*, Woodbridge (1994), 213-34.

61 Malcolm Thurlby, "'Roger of Pont l'Évêque, Archbishop of York (1154-81), and French Sources for the beginnings of Gothic architecture in Northern Britain', *England and the Continent in the Middle Ages: Studies in Memory of Andrew Martindale*, ed. John Mitchell, Stamford (2000), 35-47; Malcolm Thurlby, "Observations on the Twelfth-Century Sculpture from Bridlington Priory", *Medieval Art and Architecture in the East Riding of Yorkshire: British Archaeological Association Conference Transactions*, IX, ed. Christopher Wilson, Leeds (1989), 33-43. Christopher Wilson, "Gothic Architecture Transplanted: the Nave of the Temple Church in London", in *The Temple Church in London, History, Architecture, Art*, ed. Robin Griffith-Jones and David Park, Woodbridge (2010), 19-43.

62 Peter Draper, "The Nine Altars at Durham and Fountains", in *Medieval Art and Architecture* (1980), 74-86.

63 Georgina Russell, "The North Window of the Nine Altars Chapel, Durham Cathedral", ibid,

87-89.

64   Fernie (1994), *op. cit.* note 49.

65   McAleer (2001), *op. cit.* note 50.

66   Eric Fernie, "The Romanesque Church of Selby Abbey", in *Yorkshire Monasticism: Archaeology, Art and Architecture: British Archaeological Association Conference Transactions*, XVI, ed. Lawrence R. Hoey, Leeds (1995), 40-49; Stuart Harrison and Malcolm Thurlby, 'Observations on the Transepts, Crossing and Nave Aisles of Selby Abbey', in *ibid*, 50-61.

67   Commission on Historical Monuments, *Inventory of Historical Monuments in Westmorland*, London (1936), 133; Nikolaus Pevsner, *The Buildings of England: Cumberland and Westmorland* (Harmondsworth: Penguin Books, 1967), 18-19, 361.

68   Thurlby, *op. cit.* note 58, 277.

69   William Dugdale, *Monasticon Anglicanum*, III, London (1830), 553.

70   *VCH Cumberland*, II, 181.

71   *Domesday Book, Yorkshire*, ed. Margaret L. Faull and Marie Stinson (1986), 1Y8; *Regesta regum Anglo-Normannorum*, I, 1066-1154, ed. H.W.C Davis, Oxford (1913), CHECK #837 [1100-1107]. W/M. Notification by Henry I to Osbert the Sheriff and all the barons of Yorkshire. Giving and granting to St Peter and Gerard, Archbishop of York, the churches of Pocklington, [Gt] Driffield, Kilham, Pickering, Aldborough and Snaith with all their chapels.

72   Eric Fernie, *An Architectural History of Norwich Cathedral*, Oxford (1994), 129-33; Malcolm Thurlby, 'Articulation as an expression of function in Romanesque architecture', *Architecture and Interpretation: Essays for Eric Fernie*, Woodbridge (2012), 42-59.

73   Fernie (2000), *op. cit.* note 1, 186 with further references

74   Richard Fawcett, *The Architecture of the Scottish Medieval Church*, New Haven and London (2011), 21.

75   Eric Fernie, 'The Romanesque Churches of Dunfermline Abbey", in *Medieval Art and Architecture in the Diocese of St Andrews: British Archaeological Association Conference Transactions*, XIV, ed. John Higgitt, Leeds (1994), 25-37; Neil Cameron, "The Romanesque Sculpture of Dunfermline Abbey: Durham versus the Vicinal", *ibid*, 118-23; Fawcett (2011), *op. cit.*, note 74, 26.

76   Malcolm Thurlby, 'Aspects of the architectural history of Kirkwall Cathedral', *Proceedings of the Society of Antiquaries of Scotland*, 127 (1997), 855-88.

77   Eric Cambridge, "The early building history of St Andrews Cathedral", *Antiquaries Journal*, 57 (1977), 277-88; Malcolm Thurlby, "St Andrews Cathedral-Priory and the Beginnings of Gothic Architecture in Northern Britain", in *Medieval Art and Architecture in the Diocese of St Andrews: British Archaeological Association Conference Transactions*, XIV, ed. John Higgitt, Leeds (1994), 47-60.

78   Robert W. Billings, *Architectural Antiquities of the County of Durham*, Durham (1846).

79   Charles H. Moore, "The aisle vaulting of Winchester transept", *Journal of the Royal Institute of British Architects*, XXIII (1916), 313-20, 329-34. See also, John Crook and Yoshio Kusaba, "The Transepts of Winchester Cathedral: archaeological evidence, problems of design, and sequence of construction", *Journal of the Society of Architectural Historians*, 50 (1991), 293-310.

80   Y.M. Froidevaux, "L'abbatiale de Lessay", *Les monuments historiques de la France*, 4

(1958), 139-40.

81   For Tollvast, see Lucien Musset, *Normandie romane, I, La Basse-Normandie*, 2nd edn, La Pierre-qui-Vire, Yonne (1975), 163-67, pls 68-75.

82   William W. Clark, "The nave of Saint-Pierre at Lisieux: Romanesque structure in a Gothic guise", *Gesta*, XVI/I (1977), 29-38.

83   Gardner (1982), *op. cit.,* note 3, 577, fig. 22.

84   The importance of the decorative aspect of Romanesque Durham was emphasized by Geoffrey Webb, *Architecture in Britain: The Middle Ages*, Harmondsworth (1956), 38-39; see also, T.S.R. Boase, *English Art 1100-1216*, Oxford (1953), 21. Peter Kidson, Peter Murray and Paul Thompson, *A History of English Architecture*, Harmondsworth (1979), 53; Bony (1981), *op. cit.* note 21, 79-80. John Bilson, "The Beginnings of Gothic Architecture in England", *Journal of the Royal Institute of British Architects*, 3rd series, VI (1899), 259-269, 289-326, saw the complex arch mouldings as forerunners of English Gothic mouldings.

Chapter 3

Author's note: a few minor corrections have been made to this chapter since the second edition of 1995, and colour illustrations substituted for some of those formerly in black and white. I would like to thank Sharon Cather and Sophie Stewart for their help.

1   *Rites of Durham* (Surtees Society, 107), ed. J.T. Fowler, 1903.

2   They are briefly described by M. Johnson. 'Recent work on the refectory of Durham Cathedral', *Transactions of the Architectural and Archaeological Society of Durham and Northumberland*, new ser., 1(1968), 86-7. A fine example of a refectory scheme showing both patrons and patron saint is provided by the 13th-century and later paintings at Horsham St Faith Priory (Norfolk); see D Purcell 'The priory of Horsham St Faith and its wall paintings', *Norfolk Archaeology*, 35 (1974) 469-73 These also include an enormous Crucifixion - likewise a standard subject for refectories - and the Rites, records a similar painting (of late medieval date?) on the west wall at Durham, 'which pictures have been washed over with Lime, and yet do appear through the Lime.'

3   E. Fernie (1980), *op.cit.*, 49-58.

4   D. Park and P. Welford, 'The medieval polychromy of Winchester Cathedral', in *Winchester Cathedral: Nine Hundred Years 1093-1993*, ed. J. Crook (Chichester and Winchester 1993), 125.

5   See J. Haselock and D. O'Connor. 'The medieval stained glass of Durham Cathedral', in *Medieval Art and Architecture of Durham Cathedral*, 109.

6   The Finchale decoration has now almost disappeared, but is known e.g. from a watercolour by H.M. Office of Works date 1924 (I am grateful to David Sherlock for drawing this to my attention). At Durham itself, one further example of 13th-century polychromy deserves notice: flesh-tints and other colouring surviving on the carved angels at clerestory level in the choir, dating from the end of the century, and first noted during examination prior to cleaning of the vault in 1990.

7   See D. Park, '*Romanesque wall paintings at Ickleton*', in *Romanesque and Gothic: Essays for George Zarnecki* (Woodbridge 1987), 159-69; and S. Rickerby and D. Park, 'A Romanesque *Visitatio Sepulchri* at Kempley', *Burlington Magazine*, 133 (1991), 27-31.

[8] For the candlestick, and other metalwork which must have contributed greatly to the appearance of the cathedral (and of which the sanctuary ring and ironwork of the south-west doorway are major late 12th-century survivals), see J. Geddes, 'The twelfth-century metalwork at Durham Cathedral', in *Medieval Art and Architecture at Durham Cathedral*, 140-8, and idem. 'The sanctuary ring of Durham Cathedral', Archaeologia, 107 (1982), 125-9.

[9] See M. Camille, The Gothic Idol: Ideology and Image-making in Medieval Art, Cambridge 1989, 230-2.

[10] See C. Wilson, 'The Neville Screen', in Medieval Art and Architecture at Durham Cathedral, 90-104.

[11] All the wall paintings in this chapel are discussed in detail by D. Park, 'The wall paintings in the Galilee Chapel of Durham Cathedral', in Friends of Durham Cathedral, Fifty-seventh Annual Report, 1990, 21-34.

P. Welford, 'An investigation into the phenomenon of dark flesh areas in English medieval wall paintings' (unpubl. Diss., Conservation of Wall Painting Department, Courtauld Institute of Art, 1991), 4-9, pls. 14-17.

For the many brasses that once gleamed from the floor of the cathedral, but were mostly ripped up after the Reformation, see, e.g., J. Coales, ed., The Earliest English Brasses: Patronage, Style and Workshops 1270-1350, London, 1987. See also, A. Martindale, 'Patrons and minders: the intrusion of the secular into sacred spaces in the late Middle Ages', in The Church and the Arts (Studies in Church History, 28), ed. D. Wood, Oxford 1992, 143-78, for a useful general discussion of secular imagery in churches at this period.

[14] The paintings underwent conservation in 1983 by the Canterbury Cathedral Wallpaintings Workshop, and the above account draws heavily in its dating of the paintings and in other aspects on the Workshop's unpublished report by F. Allardyce, L. Medhurst and T. Organ. The hymn was identified by Martin Snape, and the indigo by Helen Howard ('Blue pigments in English medieval wall painting', unpubl. Diss., Conservation of Wall Painting Department, Courtauld Institute of Art, 1988, 42-3, ills. 62-9).

Chapter 4

Shortened Titles used: *ACM – Abstracts of Chapter Minutes:* Vol 1 to 1726, Vol ll 1726-1829, Vol lll 1829-67. Dean and Chapter Library. *Record – Record of works in and upon the Cathedral Church of Durham 1700-1857* and *1858-64*. Privately printed, Dean and Chapter.

1. John Harvey, English Medieval Architects 91984), 345.
2. Martin G. Snape, Medieval Art and Architecture, op. cit. 28-9.
4. *ACM* Vol l, 18th August 1631.
5. *ACM* Vol l, 6th November 1660.
6. N. Pevsner, revised E. Williamson, *op.cit.,* 119.
7. *ACM* Vol l, 5th October 1661, 185-6.
8. Conrad Eden, *Organs of Durham Cathedral* (1970), 6-7.
9. *ACM*, 582.
10. William Hutchinson, *History of Durham* (1787), first edition with plates, Vol 2, 227

11. *ACM*, 629.
12. *ACM*, 634, 20th November 1795.
13. R.W.Billings, *Architectural Illustrations and Description of the Cathedral church at Durham*, London, (1843), !4. (Billings mentions the colossal heads of the founders, William Carilef and Rufus.)
14. William Greenwell, *Durham Cathedral* (1881, 8th edition, 1913) 33.
15. *ACM*, 21st July 1806.
16. Record, XXXIV.
17. Ibid.
18. *Ibid*. (The 16th century Screen round the feretory was given to the University. In the 1930s sufficient of it had survived for it to be copied and the Screen renewed in oak round the Feretory.)
19. *Ibid*.. (The clock Case was shown in Carter's Long Section and in a Billing's ' perspective. It was reassembled and restored to its original position in 1936.)
20. *ACM*, 17th November1849
21. *Record* XXXVI . (J.C. Bishop, founder of the firm of organ builders of the name.)
22. *Record* XXXVIII and ACM 17th December 1847.
23. *ACM* 2nd November 1858.
24. *ACM* 6th March 1860. (i.e. The Chapter did not accept Scott's proposals, but wished to leave the tower as it had been.)
25. The Pelican Lectern was made for Scott in 1876 by Francis A. Skidmore of Birmingham. The design was intended to follow the description of the lectern in the *Rites of Durham*.
26. Proceedings of Soc. Antiquities London, Second Series, Vol XXVIII 1915-16, 44-56.
27. Christopher Cotton and Elizabeth Humble, *Durham Cathedral Framework Management Plan*, Purcell Architects (2012); Christopher Cotton and Alex Holton, *Durham Cathedral: The Claustral Buildings Historic buildings* Approach, Purcell Architects (2012).

Acknowledgement. Chapter 4 is largely based on the Durham Lecture, 1985, given by Ian Curry, entitled 'Sense and Sensitivity – Durham Cathedral and its Architects', and published by the Dean and Chapter of Durham in 1985.